First published in Great Britain in 2013 by The Rare Brand Market
Copyright © **The Rare Brand Market**, Emma Schwarz
Text and Recipes © 2013 **The Rare Brand Market**, Emma Schwarz
The Author, The Rare Brand Market, Emma Schwarz has asserted its rights under the Copyright, Designs and Patents Act 1988 to be identified as the author of this work.
Recipe Photography © 2013 Tory Collins.

All other photography is copyright to various individuals and businesses. Some brand photography is owned outright by the rare brands that are involved in this book. Other photography is as credited on the relevant photograph, and copyright is retained by the following photographers: Sasha Holloway (Blew Lips Photography), Charlie Birchmore, Rob Lawson, Richard Moran, Bradley Steenkamp, Alun Callender and DED Association Ltd.

The address of the publisher is Office 70, 26 The Hornet, Chichester, West Sussex, PO19 7BB.

ISBN 978 0 9926005 0 1

Printed and bound in Great Britain by PPG Print
www.ppgprint.co.uk

There are some **Notes to the Reader** that are important to read, please see those on Page 222.

The author and publisher disclaim, as far as the law allows, any liability arising directly or indirectly from the use, or misuse, of the information contained in this book. The information in this book has been compiled in a way of general guidance in relation to the specific subjects addressed, but is not a substitute and shall not be relied on for medical, healthcare, pharmaceutical or other professional advice on specific circumstances and in specific locations. So far as the author is aware the information given is correct and up to date as of June 2013. Practice, laws and regulations all change, and the reader should obtain up to date professional advice on any such issues.

www.therarebrandmarket.co.uk
www.therarebrandmarketlarder.co.uk

the rare brand market

THE RARE BRAND MARKET COOKBOOK
VOLUME I

Author and Food Stylist
Emma Schwarz
www.therarebrandmarket.co.uk

Chef and Food Consultant
Paul Collins
www.chefpaulcollins.co.uk

Food Photography (Recipes)
Tory McTernan
www.torymcternan.co.uk

Graphic Design
Atelier of Alchemy
www.atelierofalchemy.com

For my family...

MARK, LORENZA, ESTELLE AND GRETA

family [fam'e-lê] • *noun* a group of people who rely on each in common love, support and comfort.

This book has meant I've been a part of something wonderful. It's the people involved in this book that really make it. In my family, I'm already part of something very wonderful. There's nothing more special than to love and be loved for the rest of your life — no matter what.

food with stories...

it's the people that make it!

STARTERS AND CANAPÉS

Mid Summer Salmon Delight	HANSEN AND LYDERSEN
Harissa Stuffed Chicory Leaves	JAMES' FOOD
Smoked Tomato Tapenade & Parma Sticks	PINKS
Asian Crispbreads	PETER'S YARD
Pink Grapefruit & Potted Trout	POTTED GAME
Onion & Chilli Chutney Tarts	RUBIES IN THE RUBBLE
Ham Hock & Garden Pea Summer Soup	FARMISON & CO.
Crab & Asparagus Arancinis	THE REAL CO.
Vintage Cheddar Soufflés	GODMINSTER
Home Cured Citrus Sea Trout	FALKSALT

LUNCHEONS AND SUPPERS

Lavender & Apricot BBQ Chicken	MAYFIELD LAVENDER
Biltong / Cured Beef Salad	THE BILTONG COMPANY
Chorizo & Sprouting Broccoli Tortilla	PURE SPAIN
Hot Smoked Chicken Salad	THE CHESIL SMOKERY
Open Veggie Burger on Walnut & Pumpkin Seed Bread	BREAD À LA MER
Goat's Cheese & Tomato Tart	THE CHEESEBOARD
Fruity & Nutty Rice Salad with Honey Dressing	THE SHEFFIELD HONEY CO.
Black Truffle Lasagne	MISTER TRUFFLE
Oyster Mushroom Risotto	ESPRESSO MUSHROOM CO.
Lemon Infused Lamb with Apricot Israeli Couscous	THE WELL HUNG MEAT CO.

INTERESTING VEGETABLES AND PLANTS

Balsamic & Honey Glazed Carrots	LUCY'S DRESSINGS
Braised Cabbage & Blackberry Vinegar	WOMERSLEY
Manchego Stuffed Chillies	MUSWELL HILL CHEESE SHOP
White Miso Aubergines	SOUS CHEF
Raw Tofu with Soya Sauce Dressing	CLEAN BEAN
Butternut Squash, Black Bean & Feta Tacos	THE GREEK DELI
Spiced Cauliflower with Garlic Pachadi, Dhal & Chapatis	MANJIRA
Green Bean Curry	BIT SPICY
Cretan Tomato & Zucchini Potato Gratin	MESTÓ ARTISAN OLIVE OIL
Freekeh Tabouleh	TERRA ROSSA

PUDDINGS

Raw Chocolate & Orange Upside Down Cake	THE RAW CHOCOLATE CO.
British Summer Fruit Pudding	YARTY CORDIALS
Blueberry, Blackberry & Passion Fruit Pavlova	MRS DARLINGTON & DAUGHTERS
Lemon Cheesecake with Chocolate Biscotti Crust	PEACE OF CAKE LONDON
Matcha & Vanilla Cream Cake	TEA STUDIO
Beetroot, Ginger & Apple Summer Crumble	JUST INGREDIENTS
Raspberry, Fig, Pecan & Ginger Ice Cream Cake	CAROLINE'S DAIRY
Lemon & Berry Tart	ROSEBUD PRESERVES
Sticky Date Madeleines with Butterscotch Sauce	THE FUDGE KITCHEN
Granola — Knickerbocker Glory Style	SCRUMSHUS

EAT YOUR DRINK

Elderflower, Watermelon, Lime & Gin Granita	SIPSMITH
Raw Prawns with Asian Ginseng Dipping Sauce	KAMM AND SONS
BBQ Beer Chicken	BILL'S PRODUCE STORE
Sarsaparilla Vanilla Floats	MAWSON'S
Sloe Lemonade Dessert Slices	BRECKLAND ORCHARD
Espresso Infused Crème Brûlées	HORSHAM COFFEE ROASTERY
Lemon & Thyme Cookies with Earl Grey Glaze	ROSY LEE TEA
English Mead & Quince Tarte Tartin	LURGASHALL WINERY
Raspberry Vodka Sorbet	NUTMEG FINE FOODS
Crab, Chilli & Sparkling Wine Linguine	TINWOOD ESTATE

POCKET PICNICS AND SUBTLE FEASTING

Vanilla Yogurt Covered Cranberries & Goji Berries	TIMS DAIRY
Rose Water Scones	WEETONS
Kiwi, Lemon, Elderflower & Earl Grey Marmalade Muffins	JAMSMITH
Frozen Banana & Cacao Nibbles	BOOJA-BOOJA
Popcorn Lollies	PETER POPPLE'S POPCORN

ROBIN HUTSON, BOUTIQUE HOTELIER

Robin Hutson is a tireless ambassador of Action Against Hunger and champions the nation's food lovers to help prevent children from dying from malnutrition by getting involved in its 'Love Food Give Food' fundraising campaign. He is also the great British hotelier synonymous with excellence in an unstuffy way. His current stable includes the 5-star **Lime Wood** hotel and the growing brand, **The Pig**: **The Pig** – in the wall, **The Pig** – near Bath, **The Pig** – in the forest and **The Pig** – on the beach.

Robin is a man not only in tune with his customers' micro wishes but the world's macro humanitarian aid programme. A movement to end world poverty which is gaining momentum through campaigns such as 'Love Food Give Food' and the Fine Wine Auction event to support the charity Action Against Hunger. The aim of this wonderful charity is to turn the nation's culinary passion into humanitarian action and help save the lives of malnourished children and their families around the world.

A note from Robin...

Any book that supports artisan food producers, the independents food scene and puts good quality ingredients on a pedestal is a book that interests me. Add to that a book that fundraises for Action Against Hunger and you have my undivided attention.

Emma's tenacity to get this book self-published is a testament to the passion that you feel when you read through the pages of this book. It comes bursting through. I am also a big supporter of businesses trading with social responsibility and that is why I support the 'Love Food Give Food' campaign for Action Against Hunger. This links nicely to The Rare Brand Market's approach to 'giving back'... so it was a pleasure when Emma asked me to write a note to introduce The Rare Brand Cookbook.

www.lovefoodgivefood.org
www.actionagainsthunger.org.uk

A note from Emma...

We constantly strive at The Rare Brand Market to 'give back' in a lot of what we do — at our markets we like to encourage spending and giving, so we share door monies with charities along with other fundraising initiatives. For this cookbook we really wanted to support 'giving food', so it was a natural choice for me to support a worldwide hunger cause. This led us to Action Against Hunger.

It seemed especially appropriate to me that we should make the connection between the good fortune of our access to such a varied food culture and the basic nutritional needs of those world communities which have less.

Fighting hunger simply by buying a copy of a fantastic recipe book — what an excellent way to help others, not by doing something you don't like but by doing something you do. So it was a natural choice for us to support Action Against Hunger and to join their fight against worldwide malnutrition.

Robin Hutson is the perfect person to support this cookbook. Robin is fanatical about good food, great ingredients and supporting artisan food producers. He is chairperson of the charity committee for Action Against Hunger, and champion of their 'Love Food Give Food' project campaign with leading restaurants. If Robin was a rock star, I would be a groupie.

I have followed Robin's career with great admiration. It seems every hotel or restaurant he has been involved in holds a dear memory for me. The Chewton Glen in the New Forest, the marvellous Hotel du Vin Group — I think I have stayed at them all, during his long-term directorship and collaboration with Nick Jones at Soho House. I witnessed the launch of Cecconi's (my favourite place for breakfast) as well as the collection of über cool Soho House clubs and hotels scattered throughout the world. Chiswick High Road House is a London haven and the New York Soho House Hotel is the coolest hang out as well as one of the few hotels with a fab rooftop pool! I am in awe of his vision. With his recent projects at 5-star **Lime Wood** hotel and **The Pig** brand, he continues to build brands which brilliantly combine luxury with homely charm.

Robin recently won the of **Hotel Personality of the Year** award. At the ceremony he was described as a creative genius, an enigmatic visionary and the man with the Midas touch and that was an understatement. So thank you Robin for lending this book a little bit of your magic — it is a true honour.

Robin's latest ventures are always evolving, keep up-to-date with them online.

www.thepighotel.co.uk @The_Pig_Hotel
www.limewoodhotel.co.uk @limewoodhotel

ACTION AGAINST HUNGER

PETER AT THE ACTION AGAINST HUNGER NUTRITION PROGRAMME

Peter's Story...

When hunger and poverty strike, it is the young who are hit first and hardest. Peter is a three-year-old orphan from Monrovia, Liberia. Following the death of his mother he was taken on a long journey in the scorching heat to the home of his 85-year old great grandmother. By the time he arrived he was suffering from malnutrition — for this little boy it was a life threatening condition. Peter was so sick he could no longer walk, eat or even smile.

Thankfully, Peter was admitted to **Action Against Hunger**'s nutrition programme. He received emergency treatment and a supply of highly nutritious therapeutic foods to take home. His great grandmother fed him every day and nursed him back to health. A fortnight after Peter's first visit to the centre he was able to walk again. He has made a full recovery and never stops smiling.

www.actionagainsthunger.org.uk   @ACF_UK

FOR EVERY 5* RARE BRAND COOKBOOKS SOLD, ACTION AGAINST HUNGER CAN PROVIDE SOMEONE LIKE PETER WITH A WEEK'S SUPPLY OF NUTRITIONAL PRODUCTS, VITAMINS, MEDICINE & THERAPEUTIC MILK. *MIN. COST BASED ON LAUNCH RRP.

INTRODUCTION

the rare brand market

EMMA SCHWARZ, FOUNDER, THE RARE BRAND MARKET

Before I introduce the book, it seems right to acquaint you with **The Rare Brand Market** business — a little known yet exciting way of shopping.

When I moved to Sussex from London, I knew there was a market for a fresh shopping experience which would surprise and delight customers. That was the beginning of the Rare Brand Market, an exciting new way to buy things at a regularly organised marketplace. A hub of innovative ideas to celebrate the best products not found easily on any high street.

I was spurred on by the renaissance in all things independent. A rising demand for quality products, made by local or small companies, which tell a story. Customers getting a chance to engage and to meet the artisans who have made the products they are selling.

Emerging brands often go on to do great things and supporting that process has always been one of my goals with the business. I enjoy helping promote small companies by giving them a platform to show people what they do. With the internet and homogenized high streets, much of the joy has gone out of shopping. We hope we are slowly turning the tide with our **Rare Brand Market** events.

Why is the Rare Brand Market doing a Cookbook?

The reason is two-fold. With my heart I am influenced by a personal love affair with food. With my head it makes good business sense as we have had dealings with an increasing number of rare food brands and artisan producers. Since I founded the business in 2009, we have always had a mix of food, drink, fashion, beauty and gift retailers. Food and shopping go together. My best shopping experiences invariably involve a good lunch and scrummy food tastings along the way and, of course, it allows our partner brands to reach an audience that cannot always get to one of our live events.

At a **Rare Brand Christmas Market** it dawned on me when I was chatting to customers in our food hall that people do like some recipe inspiration when buying new food ingredients and rare products. I had been looking for a way to celebrate some of the culinary brands, so the cookbook fulfils these two objectives. I do not know of another cookbook celebrating the independent shopkeepers, makers and suppliers of artisan food in Great Britain — full of delicious recipes it serves as a living directory for you and your larder. There is a place for the supermarket in everyone's lives, but food shopping can be and should be more pleasurable...

"One cannot think well, love well, sleep well, if one has not dined well."
— Virginia Woolf

So, for all these reasons I am thrilled to introduce the first volume of **The Rare Brand Cook Book,** dedicated to showcasing the most interesting food companies in Great Britain. I think we have captured the current mood for a revived interest in ingredients and their provenance.

No matter where you live, the lure of good food seems to be constant; a daily portal to a better way of life. As Voltaire the French philosopher once said, "Nothing would be more tiresome than eating and drinking if God had not made them a pleasure as well as a necessity." I am in complete agreement.

My whole life I have had a close relationship with food. It is nearly impossible for me to meet anyone and not strike up a conversation without talking about food. This book is the culmination of those conversations with the growers, producers and importers I have had the pleasure of working with over the past few years.

My healthy obsession for good exciting food is constantly evolving. For me food makes life more interesting, it is a social and emotional experience. Put quite simply food has brought me joy. **My darling mum was definitely the catalyst.** Mum was a great cook, self-taught initially, but formalized through Cordon-Bleu training. Growing up she would involve me in every aspect of cooking from preparation to serving. She would visit the butcher, baker and farm shop to find the right ingredients. Mum would host family and social gatherings, 'putting on a spread' fit for a king. My strongest memory is her naughty desserts—summer fruit Pavlova and a particularly boozy chocolate torte.

When Mum was employed as private chef to a London family who holidayed on the South Coast, I remember consciously hearing the expression 'eat in season' for the first time. This was my early introduction to an appreciation of food sourcing which I stand by today. I remember mum bombing around Sussex to get a certain type of fish from coastal fishmongers or a particular ingredient from a specialist grocery.

As an adult, I worked for Marks and Spencer and learned about the business of food; Merchandising, quality control, provenance, margin management and production. My epiphany came during an event I had organised. We had hired the Trout Fishing Estate in Kent, which belonged to The Who's lead singer Roger Daltrey, and celebrity chefs Lesley Waters and Antony Worrall Thompson were booked. I watched as the fresh fish were cooked within minutes of being caught. It was all simply executed and brilliantly tasty — an insight into how good, fresh, ingredients are the key.

Trips abroad began to influence me and I got a taste for global eating; Malaysia, my first nasi goreng for breakfast; African bush cooking; the Caribbean street food in Antigua; and Italy where I ate pasta and gelati time and time again. When I met my Australian husband Mark we travelled extensively through Australia and Asia. All of his family are devoted foodies, and as Jews their love of food is steeped in religion and festival. It is just the kind of food I love best. Food with stories and provenance. My lovely mother-in-law introduced me to Jewish Penicillin - chicken soup for the soul - I just love my husband's reaction when he is served this classic dish from his childhood.

> "Worries go down better with soup." — Jewish Proverb

Eating out and enjoying food is a big thing in the Schwarz family. When we visit Australia we always try to make time to visit our two favourite family restaurants; The Pantry in Melbourne and Bill Granger in Sydney. My major connection with my late father-in-law was our shared loved of food. One of my best memories is a meal at the famous Carnegie Deli on 7 Ave/55th Street in New York — we both over-ordered but, spurring each other on, ate until the plate was clean. Or the time in Sorrento, East of Melbourne when we devoured a large plate of the world famous cannoli together.

Mark and I chose Umbria in Italy as the location for our wedding. Another culinary milestone in my food journey. Our wedding menu celebrated true Italian simplicity - hunks of parmesan with balsamic, slivers of Parma ham with melon, fresh fig and mozzarella salad, chargrilled sea bass, panacotta, Baci chocolates and Perugian petit fours. It was a faultless day and the memory of those flavours still excites me. Living in London we were regulars at Borough Market, Brick Lane Flower Market and our local Farmers' Market in Barnes seeking in-season ingredients to create great flavours. The most recent food influence was an underground dining club I joined with friends, the principles of which were to experiment and try things you had never cooked before nor had the time to practise. Check it out via 8ateclub.blogspot.co.uk

"One of the very nicest things about life is the way we must regularly stop whatever it is we are doing and devote our attention to eating."
— Luciano Pavarotti

Two further gastronomic life changing moments led to me researching and writing this book. First was a visit to the epicurean New York delicatessen, DEAN & DELUCA. This is a lesson on how to get it right. A food store, cafe, cookbook shop, grocers, bakers, deli and butchers all rolled into one — I was inspired to seek artisan producers in the UK when I returned home.

Second, hearing about the **Slow Food Movement** while eating at Isola, Knightsbridge — more seasonal, more local, more pleasure — these are the principles I hold close to my heart and which are at the very core of **The Rare Brand Cookbook**. If you don't know about the **Slow Food Movement** then please do look them up — www.slowfood.org.uk — it was ironic that the week we did the photo shoot for this book, it was the **International Slow Food Week**; a lovely coincidence.

Find a wide selection of gourmet foods, wines, kitchenware, gifts and recipes online at: **www.therarebrandmarketlarder.co.uk**

Palazzo Terranova

Mum

New York!

Denny

Slow Food®

DEAN & DELUCA

A NOTE FROM EMMA ABOUT THE RECIPES

- The recipes in this book have been chosen because I have either made the dishes personally, eaten them in a restaurant or been cooked something similar by a friend or family member. A few recipes are ones I have created from scratch!

- All of the recipes have been tested by **Paul Collins** our wonderful 'photo shoot' Professional Chef and Food Consultant. He has added his own expertise to the recipe notes and very much bought many of my concepts to life.

- I hope you will agree the recipes are 'fuss-free,' many of them are so easy because the core ingredient is 'already produced' by the rare brand involved.

- So many chefs including Paul, myself and other food professionals say good ingredients are the linchpin to any dish. So don't buy all your ingredients from the supermarket, do buy key ingredients from specialist producers because you will never regret it. Surely we should value and spend on the food we consume? And, isn't it nice to buy food with stories...?

- You will see from the **Recipe Key** below that these are things we want to draw your attention to, so please look out for them throughout the book!

- The **Quick Meal Planner** on the next few pages is also really useful when planning a dinner party to see prep, assembly and/or cook times at a quick glance.

- Please do make use of the wonderful Wine Pairing information provided by **Gulp Wines**, our rare brand wine masters — see their recommendations on each recipe page.

RECIPE KEY

script   Personal comments from Emma about the food and the rare brands

      Ingredients are Vegetarian Friendly

      Ingredients are supplied by a local, South of England food brand

      Wine recommendations by **Gulp Wines**, www.gulpwines.com — for a full listing of these wines, please refer to Pages 210 and 211.

QUICK MEAL PLANNER

30 MID SUMMER SALMON DELIGHT

PREP 10 **MINS**
ASSEMBLY 10 MINS

31 HARISSA STUFFED CHICORY LEAVES

PREP 5 **MINS**
ASSEMBLY 5 MINS

36 SMOKED TOMATO TAPENADE & PARMA STICKS

PREP 15 **MINS**
ASSEMBLY 5 MINS

37 ASIAN CRISPBREADS

PREP 10 **MINS**
ASSEMBLY 15 MINS

42 PINK GRAPEFRUIT & POTTED TROUT

PREP 10 **MINS**
ASSEMBLY 5 MINS

43 ONION & CHILLI CHUTNEY TARTS

PREP 20 **MINS**
COOK 15-20 MINS

48 HAM HOCK & GARDEN PEA SUMMER SOUP

PREP 3 **HOURS**
ASSEMBLY 5 MINS

49 CRAB & ASPARAGUS ARANCINIS

PREP 35 **MINS**
COOK 15 MINS

54 VINTAGE CHEDDAR SOUFFLÉS

PREP 35 **MINS**
COOK 10 MINS

55 HOME CURED CITRUS SEA TROUT

PREP 24 **HOURS**
PREP 10 MINS

62 LAVENDER & APRICOT BBQ CHICKEN

PREP 25 **MINS**
COOK 45 MINS

63 BILTONG / CURED BEEF SALAD

PREP 20 **MINS**
PREP 10 MINS

QUICK MEAL PLANNER

68 CHORIZO & SPROUTING
    BROCCOLI TORTILLA

    PREP 20 **MINS**
    COOK 30 MINS

69 HOT SMOKED
    CHICKEN SALAD

    PREP 30 **MINS**
    ASSEMBLY 10 MINS

74 VEGGIE BURGER ON WALNUT
    & PUMPKIN SEED BREAD

    PREP 40 **MINS**
    COOK 10 MINS

75 GOATS CHEESE
    & TOMATO TART

    PREP 20 **MINS**
    COOK 25 MINS

80 FRUITY & NUTTY RICE SALAD
    WITH HONEY DRESSING

    PREP 20 **MINS**
    COOK 10 MINS

81 BLACK TRUFFLE LASAGNE

    PREP 50 **MINS**
    COOK 40 MINS

86 OYSTER MUSHROOM
    RISOTTO

    PREP 10 **MINS**
    COOK 40 MINS

87 LEMON INFUSED LAMB
    WITH ISRAELI COUSCOUS

    PREP 10 **MINS**
    COOK 2 HOURS

94 BALSAMIC & HONEY
    GLAZED CARROTS

    PREP 15 **MINS**
    COOK 45 MINS

95 BRAISED CABBAGE &
    BLACKBERRY VINEGAR

    PREP 20 **MINS**
    COOK 40 MINS

100 MANCHEGO STUFFED
    CHILLIES

    PREP 20 **MINS**
    COOK 10 MINS

101 WHITE MISO AUBERGINES

    PREP 20 **MINS**
    COOK 25 MINS

QUICK MEAL PLANNER

**106 RAW TOFU WITH
SOYA SAUCE DRESSING**

PREP 10 MINS
ASSEMBLY 5 MINS

**107 BUTTERNUT SQUASH,
BLACK BEAN & FETA TACOS**

PREP 20 MINS
ASSEMBLY 10 MINS

**112 SPICED CAULIFLOWER WITH
PACHADI, DHAL & CHAPATIS**

PREP 15 MINS
COOK 20 MINS

113 GREEN BEAN CURRY

PREP 15 MINS
COOK 25 MINS

**118 CRETIAN TOMATO &
ZUCCHINI POTATO GRATIN**

PREP 1 HOUR

119 FREEKEH TABOULEH

PREP 45 MINS
COOK 35 MINS

**126 RAW CHOCOLATE & ORANGE
UPSIDE DOWN CAKE**

PREP 30 MINS
COOK 1 HR 30 MINS

**127 BRITISH SUMMER FRUIT
PUDDING**

PREP 24 HOURS
COOK 15 MINS

**132 BLUEBERRY, BALCKBERRY &
PASSION FRUIT PAVLOVA**

PREP 40 MINS
COOK 50 MINS

**133 LEMON CHEESECAKE WITH
CHOCOLATE BISCOTTI CRUST**

PREP 2 HRS 30 MINS
ASSEMBLY 30 MINS

**138 MATCHA & VANILLA
CREAM CAKE**

PREP 1 HOUR
COOK 45 MINS

**139 BEETROOT, GINGER &
APPLE SUMMER CRUMBLE**

PREP 40 MINS
COOK 30 MINS

QUICK MEAL PLANNER

QUICK MEAL PLANNER

144 RASBERRY, FIG, PECAN & GINGER ICE CREAM CAKE

PREP 24 HOURS
ASSEMBLY 20 MINS

145 LEMON & BERRY TART

PREP 20 MINS
COOK 10 MINS

150 STICKY DATE MADELEINES WITH BUTTERSCOTCH SAUCE

PREP 24 HOURS
COOK 10 MINS

151 GRANOLA KNICKERBOCKER GLORY STYLE

PREP 30 MINS
COOK 10 MINS

158 ELDERFLOWER, WATERMELON, LIME & GIN GRANITA

PREP 24 HOURS
ASSEMBLY 5 MINS

159 RAW PRAWNS WITH ASIAN GINSENG DIPPING SAUCE

PREP 24 HOURS
ASSEMBLY 10 MINS

164 BBQ BEER CHICKEN

PREP 30 MINS
COOK 30 MINS

165 SARSAPARILLA VANILLA FLOATS

PREP 2 MINS
COOK 2 MINS

170 SLOE LEMONADE DESSERT SLICES

PREP 35 MINS
COOK 45 MINS

171 ESPRESSO INFUSED CRÈME BRÛLÉES

PREP 5 HOURS
COOK 20 MINS

176 LEMON & THYME COOKIES WITH EARL GREY GLAZE

PREP 1 HR 20 MINS
COOK 20 MINS

177 ENGLISH MEAD & QUINCE TARTE TARTIN

PREP 45 MINS
COOK 45 MINS

QUICK MEAL PLANNER

182 RASPBERRY VODKA
SORBET

PREP 2 HRS 20 MINS
ASSEMBLY 5 MINS

183 CRAB, CHILLI & SPARKLING
WINE LINGUINE

PREP 20 MINS
COOK 20 MINS

190 YOGURT CRANBERRIES
& GOJI BERRIES

PREP 6 HOURS
ASSEMBLY 5 MINS

191 ROSE WATER SCONES

PREP 15 MINS
COOK 10 MINS

196 ELDERFLOWER & EARL
GREY MARMALADE MUFFINS

PREP 20 MINS
COOK 20 MINS

197 FROZEN BANANA &
RAW CACAO NIBBLIES

PREP 1 HR 40 MINS
ASSEMBLY 5 MINS

202 POPCORN LOLLIES

PREP 25 MINS
ASSEMBLY 5 MINS

Photography: Hansen and Lydersen

STARTERS AND CANAPÉS

Mid Summer Salmon Delight
HANSEN AND LYDERSEN

Harissa Stuffed Chicory Leaves
JAMES' FOOD

Smoked Tomato Tapenade & Parma Sticks
PINKS

Asian Crispbreads
PETER'S YARD

Pink Grapefruit & Potted Trout
POTTED GAME

Onion & Chilli Chutney Tarts
RUBIES IN THE RUBBLE

Ham Hock & Garden Pea Summer Soup
FARMISON & CO.

Crab & Asparagus Arancinis
THE REAL CO.

Vintage Cheddar Soufflés
GODMINSTER

Home Cured Citrus Sea Trout
FALKSALT

HANSEN AND LYDERSEN

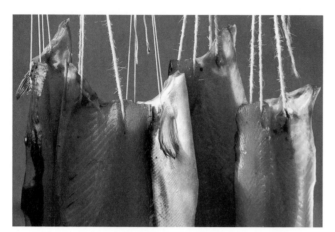  

This is the story of a tall, Norwegian man who has made it his mission to sell one product rather well. Ole Hansen brought his great-grandfather's smoked salmon recipe to a tiny, brick smokery on the back of a converted semi-industrial building in London.

In 1886, Lyder-Nilsen was a fisherman in Kirkenes, a small town 240 miles north of the Arctic Circle. "Inside my smoking chamber," explains Ole, "I have to re-create the humidity and temperature of Kirkenes and subject our salmon to an Arctic strong wind by keeping it moving throughout the smoking process."

This helps the taste migrate through the flesh of the fish and allows 100% pure juniper and beech wood flour and chips, from smoked products specialist Dansk Traeme, to infuse and flavour.

Like a bakery Hansen-Lydersen smoke the salmon every day and only to order. They use the freshest fish and smoke it for a minimum of ten hours within 48 hours of it being alive and swimming. "I can hang around 50 sides here," says Hansen, pointing out the domestic fans that circulate the smoke and the tiny fan heater that keeps the humidity down.

"All of this stuff is connected to a computer so I can control it from my iPhone. I want to establish a network of local fishermen in Norway, take their photographs and offer people the ability to choose their own fisherman. You'll know the actual guy who catches the fish you've ordered. You'll be able to look on Google Earth and see exactly where he's fishing."

Surely this is food provenance at its purest.

www.hansen-lydersen.com

serve with vodka shots — a
brilliant way to get any
party started!

MID SUMMER SALMON DELIGHT

PREP 10 MINS   ASSEMBLY 10 MINS

INGREDIENTS (STARTER FOR 4)

½ HANSEN AND LYDERSEN SMOKED SALMON
SODA BREAD OR LOAF OF SOUR DOUGH
CRÈME FRAICHE
FRESH DILL

METHOD (STARTER)

- Thickly slice smoked salmon on to generous portions of soda bread or sour dough.
- Fan as shown in the picture (above left).
- Add a dollop of crème fraiche and top with a sprig of dill.

GULP WINES RECOMMEND...

Domaine de Guillemarine Picpoul
2011

PREP 10 MINS   ASSEMBLY 10 MINS

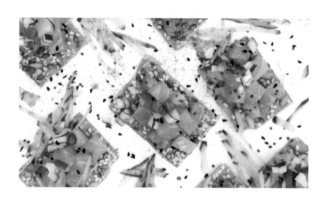

INGREDIENTS (SERVES 10)

½ HANSEN AND LYDERSEN SMOKED SALMON
I TSP MUSTARD SEEDS
I TSP NIGELLA SEEDS
I PACK OF SEEDED CRACKERS*
½ CUCUMBER, FINELY CHOPPED
I RED ONION, FINELY CHOPPED
½ SMALL JAR OF CAPERS

METHOD (CANAPÉ)

- Mix finely chopped salmon, cucumber, red onion and capers in a bowl, then transfer neatly onto crackers (*we recommend Dr Karg Seeded Crackers).
- Sprinkle with mustard seeds and Nigella seeds.

HARISSA STUFFED CHICORY LEAVES

PREP *5* **MINS**   **ASSEMBLY** *5* **MINS**

INGREDIENTS

**CHICORY LEAVES, NICE GREEN LEAVES
JAMES' FOOD "HARISSA DIP"**

METHOD

- Generously place James' Food Harissa Dip in chicory leaves.
- Style as you wish.
- Do not fill too early as the oil will run. So, as a canapé, you should be preparing and serving almost at the same time.

GULP WINES RECOMMEND...

Auramaris Vermentino

2011

JAMES' FOOD

James' Food

James' Food was founded in 2012 by Bristol foodie James Purslow. While studying in Liverpool he was a frequent customer at a small North African restaurant which served a fantastic starter — toasted bread and Harissa dip. In his own kitchen, James spent several years trying to perfect that memorable dip. He experimented with all the recipes he could find until finally creating the perfect Harissa balance.

The dip ended up just right - not too hot not too hot but still alive with traditional and subtle North African flavours. Loved by friends it was time to share it with as many people as possible. So armed with his one Harissa dip James nervously launched his business at the Love Food Festival. "There'll be lots of stalls possibly looking more professional and certainly more variety of offerings. My one dip will be making me feel slightly inadequate, but does size matter?" he wrote on his blog.

It was a success. Not content on being a one trick pony though, James realised Harissa was just the beginning and he needed a couple more flavours to satisfy his customers' wide ranging taste buds. He worked with existing recipes and gave them his own twists and tweaks developing a range of handmade dips including the creamy and subtle Nutty Butter Bean and the fresh and zesty Twisted Tapenade to sell alongside the original intense fiery Moreish Harissa.

www.james-food.com

PINK'S

Spearheaded by Fiona Pink, PINK'S, the award-winning food producer, holds traditional values at their very core and have been inspired by family tradition. PINK'S Jam & Pickle Factory was founded in the late 1880s in Bermondsey, South London. The firm originally supplied pickles, jams, confectionary, Italian goods, candied peels and spices. With PINK'S great grandfather at the helm, the company became a household name and secured a contract to supply PINK'S Plum Jam to the troops during the Great War. PINK'S was said to be the largest manufacturer of marmalade in the world. Records show during the year of 1897 they produced 3,400 tons of marmalade requiring 1,950 tons of oranges and 1,800 tons of sugar.

There was an ethos to supply food that was pure and untainted and it is the driving focus behind the company today. PINK'S are passionate about using only the very finest, freshest ingredients — locally sourced wherever possible. All their products are made by hand in small batches, using open pans to ensure their quality.

PINK'S has been recognised for the outstanding quality of their products — their Oak Smoked Sweet Peppers and Lime & Lemongrass Green Chilli have both received Gold at the Great Taste Awards. Their Smoked Tomato Tapenade won a prestigious Gold in the Taste of the West, with Silver going to their Ginger & Garlic Red Chilli Jelly.

PINK'S delicious range also includes Red Chilli Jelly, Oak Smoked Cherry Tomatoes, Oven Roasted Cherry Tomatoes, Smoked Tomato Pasta Sauce and Rapeseed Oil. Each jar comes with a host of mouth watering serving suggestions, giving a twist to casseroles and risottos, ideal for dunking a large Thai prawn or simply savouring on warm buttery toast.

The temptation with PINK'S is to open up a jar and keep it to yourself!

www.pinksfoods.co.uk

SMOKED TOMATO TAPENADE & PARMA STICKS

PREP 15 **MINS**   ASSEMBLY 5 MINS

INGREDIENTS (SERVES 4-8)

1 JAR PINK'S "SMOKED TOMATO" TAPENADE
8 SLICES OF PARMA HAM
1 PACK OF ITALIAN GRISSINI STICKS

METHOD

- Halve the Parma ham, then wrap around the sticks.

- Always start with the fat at the same place on the breadsticks to ensure that they all look uniform. Use the image above for guidance.

- Serve with the smoked tomato dip along side.

GULP WINES RECOMMEND...

Parva Res Cataratto

2011

ASIAN CRISPBREADS

PREP 10 **MINS**   **ASSEMBLY** 10 **MINS**

INGREDIENTS (SERVES 6-12)

12 PETER'S YARD "CRISPBREADS"	FINELY CHOPPED CORIANDER
½ RED PEPPER	½ TSP SOY SAUCE
2 SPRING ONIONS	½ TSP LIME JUICE
2 CARROTS	¼ TSP SESAME OIL
SMALL HANDFUL MANGE TOUT	2 TBSP EITHER HOISIN SAUCE
SMALL HANDFUL CHINESE LETTUCE	- OR BALSAMIC GLAZE

METHOD

- Chop all of the vegetable contents very finely. Combine the pepper, spring onion, carrots, mange tout and cabbage into a medium-sized bowl.

- Add the soy sauce, lime juice and the sesame oil and hoisin/balsamic glaze.

- Then sprinkle with chopped coriander, before giving the bowl another mix.

- Carefully place about a tablespoon of the mixture on to each cracker.

- Serve straight away.

Cut the veg in advance and keep in the fridge. Dress at the last minute possible so that it stays nice and crunchy on the crispbreads.

GULP WINES RECOMMEND...

Julian Schaal Chardonnay

2011

PETER'S YARD

The journey of Peter's Yard started in Sweden with a late night conversation after dinner with friends. While gathered around the table, Peter asked, "Why is it so hard to find a good loaf of bread?" Little did he know where this simple question would lead him.

After many more discussions, and with the expert guidance of Swedish master baker Jan Hedh, Peter and his friends opened their own bakery in Southern Sweden. Built within a typical Skånegård with a wood-fired stone oven, the artisan bakers kneaded dough under the rafters, using only traditional methods and authentic recipes.

Sometimes it is the simplest ideas that capture hearts and minds. This bakery became more popular than Peter and his friends could ever have imagined and is still serving customers with warm, freshly baked sourdough bread baked in the same way today.

When Peter left his native Sweden to start his artisan bakery in the UK, he brought with him naturally fermenting sourdough, traditional Swedish recipes and the help of good friends. He also bought a deep respect for craftsmanship and the belief that making anything properly brings out the best in people.

Today, Peter's Yard bakes a range of traditional Swedish breads, cakes and pastries as well as their artisan crispbreads, which are now available across the UK. "We always use all-natural ingredients, traditional craft methods and work with people who do a few things very well," says Peter. "No shortcuts, no compromises. Nothing added but skill."

www.petersyard.com

POTTED GAME

Rory Baxter is a Michelin trained professional chef who works privately across Europe. He is based in Gloucestershire and runs a variety of eccentric yet successful culinary businesses. Jemima Palmer-Tomkinson turned a well-earned reputation as an outstanding cook into a job and spent two summers as head chef at Gordon Castle on the Spey. Long hours in the kitchen and an ever changing house full of guests led to many culinary experiments, some memorable some less so. Towards the end of her time on the Spey Jemima stumbled upon an old recipe that used potting as a preservation method for meat. The idea for The Potted Game Company took shape.

This is a partnership between these two young, talented chefs who are united by a shared love of British food and indeed all things edible - especially produce foraged from the wild. During their cooking careers they have both been devoted to sourcing obscure ingredients from the pastures, woodlands and hedgerows surrounding their homes. The idea of making the most of under-appreciated birds and animals appealed to Rory's long held belief in the quality of unusual British produce.

The pair set up shop at one of Rory's mobile kitchens and spent a great deal of time potting, packing and tinkering with ingredients until a small range of recipes were perfected. Potted Game has since gathered momentum at a remarkable pace, winning awards and lavish praise from professional foodies and amateur gourmands alike. The range of potted preserves can now be found weekly at Borough Market and in the food-halls of Selfridges, Fortnum and Mason and ever increasing number of farm shops, delis and other independent retailers around the country.

www.pottedgame.com

such a simple starter or canapé...

PINK GRAPEFRUIT & POTTED TROUT

PREP 10 **MINS**   ASSEMBLY 5 MINS

INGREDIENTS (SERVES 6-8)

1 POTTED GAME "TROUT POT"
1 PINK GRAPEFRUIT, SEGMENTED
½ A BUNCH OF CHIVES, CHOPPED

METHOD

- For the canape these look brilliant in shot glasses, layer the slices of grapefruit at the bottom. Top with the Trout Pot.

- Decorate with chopped chives. You can leave the chives whole if you fancy more of a 'spiked' look.

GULP WINES RECOMMEND...

Chamonix Blanc

2011

ONION & CHILLI CHUTNEY TARTS

PREP 20 **MINS**   **COOK** 15-20 MINS

INGREDIENTS (STARTER FOR 4 / CANAPÉS FOR 10)

1 RUBIES IN THE RUBBLE "RED ONION & CHILLI CHUTNEY"
1 GOAT'S CHEESE LOG
200G READYMADE ALL BUTTER PASTRY
2 TBSP PINE NUTS
1 PINCH DRIED THYME
1 EGG YOLK

METHOD

- Pre-heat the oven to 200°C / Fan 180°C / Gas 6.
- Cut the pastry into squares (15cm for a starter and 5cm for a canapé) and put a large dollop of the chutney into the centre then even out.
- Place a slice of goats cheese on top.
- Brush the edges of the squares with an egg yolk (rather than a whole egg mix), to get a really lovely shiny edge.
- Put in the oven for 15-20 minutes, or until crisp golden brown around the edges.
- Scatter with pine nuts and thyme, serve warm with a drizzle of olive oil.

serves 10 as canapés or 4 as a starter!

GULP WINES RECOMMEND...
Calusari Pinot Grigio
2011

RUBIES IN THE RUBBLE

Preserve. At Rubies in the Rubble, they love that word. Not just because preserves are what they make, by hand and with care, in the form of chutneys, jams and pickles, but also because it sums up their mission statement — to preserve, to serve, to save.

Each jar is packed with fresh fruit and veg goodness almost all of which would have otherwise gone to waste. Western countries produce up to 300% more food than they actually need, while 1 billion people suffer from malnutrition. It just doesn't seem to make sense.

Rubies in the Rubble decided to view food waste not as a cause for despair but as an exciting opportunity to create a positive and sustainable enterprise. By employing Londoners who are struggling to get back into the workplace to make the chutneys, they tackle the unemployment problem with the food surplus problem.

They strongly believe in the dignity, self-worth and responsibility involved in producing something which has value to someone else. This sustainable, profitable business produces a high-end product. At its heart Rubies in the Rubble wants to prove their produce and their people can be made precious if only given the chance.

The purpose-built kitchen at New Spitalfields wholesale fruit and veg market means they are ideally situated to intercept any unsold surplus directly to make the jam and chutney. 700,000 tons of fresh produce pass through this market every year producing over 200 tons of general waste per week. They also work directly with UK growers, making use of unwanted produce at various points in the supply chain. Their entire business model is based on a few core beliefs. Make use of what you have. Believe in people. Care about your resources. Pretty simple really…

www.rubiesintherubble.com

FARMISON & CO.

At Farmison & Co. everything they do is driven by taste and underpinned by their ethics. Founded by Lee Simmonds and John Pallagi, and shortlisted for the Grocer Awards Online Food Retailer of the Year Awards, Farmison & Co. is leading the fight for more accountability in the food chain towards a tastier and more sensible way of doing things.

As restaurateurs, Lee and John were fed up with compromising on quality and range when it came to buying food in the supermarket. Using their contacts, they sourced the same artisan made and grown produce you might expect to find in top restaurants and decided to bring it to the wider public, Farmison & Co. was born. Regardless of your whereabouts in the UK, you can now order online affordable rare and native breed meat, fresh chef-quality fruit and vegetables and Farmison & Co.'s delectable range of cheeses and luxury pantry items.

Part of the mission to widen access to the best produce is to help preserve our agricultural heritage by giving independent farmers a fair price, encouraging sustainable practices and only using rare and native breeds of lamb, beef and pork.

The benefits of being traditional about food are manifold. For starters, there's no chance of anything unwanted ending up in the meat supply chain, since the journey from pasture to plate is so short. Processed meat by nature is the supermarket's way of making more money out of natural foods, bringing it from afar, divvying it up and making it more lucrative. These reconstituted foods often have poor nutritional value.

Farmison & Co. do not squeeze their produce for profit, it comes to your door in its natural state — whole, extremely tasty, and nutritious. Unlike industrially reared animals, which are bred to get as big as possible as quick as possible, the herds that supply Farmison & Co. are allowed to mature at their own pace which makes for exceptional cooking. The difference to food abiding by Farmison & Co.'s principles are remarkable.

www.farmison.com

serve with vodka shots – a
brilliant way to get any
party started!

HAM HOCK & GARDEN PEA SUMMER SOUP

PREP 3 **HOURS**   **ASSEMBLY** 5 **MINS**

INGREDIENTS (SERVES 4)

1.25 KG FARMISON & CO.
"HAM SHANK"
1 ONION, HALVED
A BAY LEAF
100 G UNSALTED BUTTER
100 G SLICED SHALLOTS

10 CLOVES OF GARLIC
500 ML HAM* OR VEG STOCK
20 G MINT LEAVES
50 ML GROUNDNUT OIL
400 G FROZEN GARDEN PEAS

METHOD

- Soak Farmison & Co. (1.25 kg) ham shank overnight in plain water. The next day, put it on the hob with fresh water, one halved onion and a bay leaf and cook for three hours on a simmer.

- Leave your peas to defrost.

- Blanch the mint leaves in water for half a minute, take out and place in ice cold water place then transfer to a liquidiser with the oil. Then strain the oil through a sieve and save for serving.

GULP WINES RECOMMEND...

The Architect
2011 Chardonnay

- Melt half of the butter in a saucepan and then add the shallots and the garlic. Add the *ham stock (from cooking the ham) or vegetable stock and leave to simmer before adding ¾ of the peas and rest of the butter. Liquidise this (you can use a hand-held one if easier).

- Pass the soup through a sieve, mushing down the solids to extract all of the juices, into a new saucepan.

- Whizz through the hand-held blender again to make sure the soup is beautifully creamy.

- Tear and then add your tender ham hock and the rest of the peas.

- Serve in four warm bowls and drizzle over the oil prepared earlier. Add shredded ham for decoration.

CRAB & ASPARAGUS ARANCINIS

PREP 35 **MINS**   **COOK** 15 **MINS**

INGREDIENTS (MAKES 20)

200 G THE REAL CO.
"BASMATI RICE", UNCOOKED
200 G CRAB (50/50)
2 EGGS
4 WHITE SCALLIONS,
PARTLY CHOPPED

100 G MINIATURE ASPARAGUS
2 TBSP SESAME OIL
2 CLOVES OF GARLIC
3 TBSP CHIVES, CHOPPED
200 G PANKO BREADCRUMBS
SEA SALT & PEPPER

METHOD

- Pre-heat oven to 200°C / Fan 180°C / Gas 6.

- Mix the crab meat, eggs, rice, scallions and 1 tbsp. sesame oil in a bowl.

- In a separate bowl, mix the chives and panko breadcrumbs. Take a handful of the crab mixture and form it into a small ball and roll in the panko mixture.

- Repeat this until the mixture is all used and then bake for 15 minutes. Blanch the asparagus for 2 minutes in boiling water.

- Whilst this is baking, pre-heat the remaining sesame oil and crushed garlic in a griddle (or a normal frying pan will do).

- Turn asparagus until cooked but still crunchy. Season with sea salt and pepper and place on to a hot serving dish. Serve the crab balls on top.

- Alternatively, for a smaller canapé sized dish, serve a few Arancini with natural yoghurt dip sprinkled with mint. Or you can make a more substantial raita style dip by combining: 100 ml yoghurt, 100 ml diced cucumber, 50 g diced shallot, 1 small garlic clove, 5 g finely shredded mint, a squeeze of lemon and season.

GULP WINES RECOMMEND...

The Architect
2011 Chardonnay

STARTERS AND CANAPÉS

THE REAL CO.

For The Real Co. single sourcing is not just a slogan it is the way they do business. They deliver the highest quality produce in the world, sourced ethically and delivered to consumers who can see exactly where it came from and who grew it. The suppliers come from single farms, estates and cooperatives.

Until a few decades ago, the public knew where their food came from. Meals were made from scratch using local produce, so the quality was reliable. Changes in lifestyle and farming methods have led to massive differences in the way we eat - with the arrival of ready meals and fast food eating became less about goodness and more about speed and choice. It wasn't long before we became completely disconnected from the source and quality of our food.

Now allergies, health issues, obesity and ethical concerns have left consumers asking exactly what are they putting in their mouths. A discerning public want answers. Where does your food come from? Is it healthy and of good quality? Who are the growers? Do workers on the farms or plantations have fair pay and working conditions? Are pesticides or harmful chemicals used on the farms?

The Real Co. believe single sourcing answers these important questions. They work directly with a few selected organic farmers and growers across the globe, visiting growers and getting to know them. In a world where the origin and quality of most products is untraceable, their commitment to the quality of the food they sell stands out.

For example, most rice consumed worldwide is imported from India and Pakistan. Consumers have no idea how it is farmed or what harmful chemicals are used. Single sourcing enables The Real Co. to label a bag of rice with the exact farm and harvest it came from. So the consumer knows the true origin of their food and that it was farmed organically, safely and ethically with premium quality in mind.

www.thereal.co

GODMINSTER

Records show there has been a dairy farm at Godminster in Somerset for over 100 years. Life here is governed by a healthy respect for tradition and an enterprising spirit of innovation. "This applies equally to the manner in which we farm," explains farmer Richard Hollingbery, "and subsequently in determining what we should produce. You could say that we're bringing tradition up-to-date."

Godminster farm became certified organic in 1999 and decided cheddar cheese made the best use of the milk. They are complete purists when it comes to their vintage organic cheddar which is reflected in the taste.

The aim at Godminster is to create a self-sustaining environment where nature can regenerate and flourish, rather than erode, the delicate ecosystem from the effects of artificial, intensive farming. Over the last decade, they have created and restored numerous natural habitats and reintroduced native species to replenish this ecosystem. The ideal is to become entirely self-sufficient. The essential raw ingredients that are grown determine what products can be made and have led them to a vodka range which is flavoured with blackcurrant, elderflower and horseradish. Everything grown at Godminster is certified organic by the Soil Association, who inspect the farm at least once a year.

The UK government says organic farming is kinder to wildlife and the environment, causes lower contamination from sprays, has a lower carbon footprint and produces less dangerous waste — and the farmers at Godminster agree.

www.godminster.com

Tip... If you find you have made too much, turn the soufflé's out, save it for tomorrow and just re-bake!

VINTAGE CHEDDAR SOUFFLÉS

PREP 35 **MINS**   **COOK** 10 **MINS**

INGREDIENTS (STARTER FOR 4)

100 G GODMINSTER
"VINTAGE CHEDDAR", GRATED
50G UNSALTED BUTTER, PLUS
EXTRA MELTED BUTTER FOR
GREASING
40 G PLAIN FLOUR

HANDFUL OF BREADCRUMBS
½ TSP MUSTARD POWDER
½ TSP CAYENNE PEPPER
300ML MILK
4 LARGE FREE RANGE
EGGS, SEPARATED

METHOD

- Preheat oven to 200°C / Fan 180°C / Gas 6. Place a baking tray in the oven to warm up. Grease the ramekin dishes with butter and sprinkle with breadcrumbs.

- Make a simple béchamel sauce by melting the butter in the pan and add the flour, mustard powder and cayenne pepper. Cook through for a few minutes, then add the milk bit by bit, stirring until the mix comes to the boil. Boil for a few more minutes until thickened and lifting away from the sides of the pan.

- Take the pan off the heat and add the cheese, egg yolks and season.

- In another bowl, whisk the egg whites until stiff. Gradually fold the egg whites into the cheese mixture, and once combined, transfer into the ramekin dishes until it reaches the top.

- Just make sure the edge of the ramekin is clean (use a finger or tea towel).

- Transfer onto the baking tray and bake for 8-10 minutes until risen and golden.

- Serve immediately.

GULP WINES RECOMMEND...

Alain Geoffroy Chardonnay
2011

HOME CURED CITRUS SEA TROUT

PREP 24 **HOURS**   **ASSEMBLY** 10 **MINS**

INGREDIENTS (CANAPÉS FOR 20)

**400G SIDE OF SEA TROUT, SCALED & BONED – LEAVE SKIN ON
4 TBSP CITRON FALKSALT
1 TBSP CASTER SUGAR
1 LIME (ZEST & JUICE)**

METHOD

- Wash fish and remove any remaining bones. Lay skin down on a large dish.
- Grate the lime and combine this with the caster sugar and the Citron salt. Generously rub the mix over the fish. Squeeze over the fish the juice of one lime. Wrap it tightly in cling film.
- Chill for at least 24 hours, or 48 hours if you like your fish really salty. Turn over half way through.
- When ready to serve, unwrap and rinse the fish, draining away the excess liquid. Using a sharp knife, slice as thinly as possible at a slightly diagonal angle.
- Serve with vodka shots — a brilliant way to get any party started.

Goes well with cucumber and lemon, you can make a simple dressing using these ingredients and adding a little splash of olive oil, it then becomes a dressing or dipping sauce.

GULP WINES RECOMMEND...

Karl Johner Rivaner

2011

serve with vodka shots – a brilliant way to get any party started!

FALKSALT

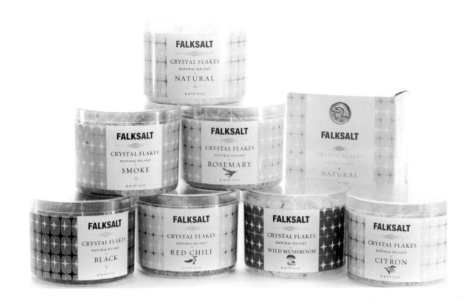

Swedish brand, Falksalt, has been making salt since 1830. They use the same combination of heat and time that fishermen stumbled on centuries ago. Building on this heritage of traditional local sea salt production our Cypriot craftsmen have perfected their techniques in order to create the finest Sea Salt crystals available. Falksalt Crystal Flakes are flake salt made from pure Mediterranean sea water. The delicate harvesting process keeps them looking gorgeous and they are soft enough to crush and flake over a finished dish.

The pure, white crystals are dried in the Mediterranean sun to an optimum moisture level whereupon natural flavourings, herbs and spices are gently toiled in by hand. The flavouring adheres to the many facets of the crystal resulting in a unique taste experience where the accented flavour combines with the gentle sea salt taste released to the palette with each mouthful of food. Accordingly, we recommend the flakes are used when ready to serve or towards the end of the cooking cycle. Falksalt Mediterranean Sea Salt Flakes from Cyprus are available in the following flavours: Natural, Black, Rosemary, Citron, Wild Garlic, Wild Mushroom, Chilli, Smoke and Chipotle.

There is a health advantage to using Falksalt Crystal Flakes sea salt too. Less salt is used, but more taste is delivered. This means that the overall usage of salt is being reduced. The salt will not be hidden inside the dish - rather it will be a more active ingredient.

www.falksalt.co.uk

Photography: Mayfield Lavender

LUNCHEONS AND SUPPERS

Lavender & Apricot BBQ Chicken
MAYFIELD LAVENDER

Biltong / Cured Beef Salad
THE CHICHESTER BILTONG COMPANY

Chorizo & Sprouting Broccoli Tortilla
PURE SPAIN

Hot Smoked Chicken Salad
THE CHESIL SMOKERY

Open Veggie Burger on Walnut & Pumpkin Seed Bread
BREAD À LA MER

Goat's Cheese & Tomato Tart
THE CHEESEBOARD

Fruity & Nutty Rice Salad with Honey Dressing
THE SHEFFIELD HONEY COMPANY

Black Truffle Lasagne
MISTER TRUFFLE

Oyster Mushroom Risotto
ESPRESSO MUSHROOM COMPANY

Lemon Infused Lamb with Apricot Israeli Couscous
THE WELL HUNG MEAT COMPANY

MAYFIELD LAVENDER

Looking out across the 25 acres of hazy blue fields at Mayfield Lavender Farm you could easily be in Provence. A family run business, less than 15 miles from Central London, Lavender has been grown in these exact fields since the eighteenth century.

The company was started when owner Brendan Maye was employed at Wella UK. He acquired the site himself after a boardroom decision left its future in jeopardy. Having made the commitment he then had the dilemma of what was involved in farming 25 acres of organic lavender and who would manage it while he continued his day job. Luckily his wife Lorna came to the rescue. It was Lorna's heroic commitment during the summers of 2006 and 2007 that sustained the project. She quickly learned how to manage and harvest lavender as well as all the logistics of co-ordinating the distillation and the product sales from the field.

At the end of the season the lavender is harvested, distilled and made into a range of toiletries. Aside from its beautiful smell and colour, Lavender is a versatile plant which has been used for its healing properties for over 2,500 years and is commonly used today as a natural antiseptic and for its anti-scarring properties. Also, as part of the mint family, it can be used to cook both savoury and sweet dishes.

"We grow three varieties of lavender - Folgate, Maillette and Grosso," explains Lorna. "It is grown without pesticides, just like it was in Victorian times." The site was awarded Soil Association Status in 2009 and, to promote biodiversity, native wildflowers have been planted around the perimeter of the fields. Brendan and Lorna now work together to nurture and build Mayfield Lavender.

www.mayfieldlavender.com

LAVENDER & APRICOT BBQ CHICKEN

PREP 5 **MINS**   **COOK** 15 **MINS**

INGREDIENTS (SERVES 4)

4 CHICKEN BREASTS, HALVED
3 TBSP MEAD OR SWEET WINE
MAYFIELD "ORGANIC FOLGATE
ENGLISH LAVENDER OIL"
1 TSP DRIED LAVENDER FLOWERS
5 TBSP APRICOT JAM
50 G DRIED APRICOTS, CHOPPED

FOR THE SAUCE

HANDFUL OF TOASTED PINE NUTS
3 TBSP CHOPPED PARSLEY
2 TBSP OLIVE OIL
2 TBSP HONEY

METHOD

- Pour the mead / sweet wine into a saucepan, add the lavender flowers, lavender oil, apricot jam and diced apricots and bring to the boil. Simmer for 2 minutes and then leave to stand.
- Preheat oven to 200°C / Fan 180°C / Gas 6. Place the chicken in a pan and coat with the lavender and apricot mixture, then roast for 45 minutes until golden brown. Set aside.
- In a bowl mix the nuts, parsley, olive oil, honey, and add some of the remaining chicken juices to taste.
- Season and serve the chicken straight away with plenty of the sauce on top.

GULP WINES RECOMMEND...

The Architect
2011 Chardonnay

BILTONG / CURED BEEF SALAD

PREP 20 **MINS**   ASSEMBLY 5 MINS

INGREDIENTS (SERVES4)

200 G MOIST "SIMPLY ORIGINAL"
BILTONG
200 G GOAT'S CHEESE
I BABY GEM LETTUCE
30 G FRESH CORIANDER
4-5 FRESH OR PICKLED FIGS*
HANDFUL OF CASHEW NUTS

FOR THE DRESSING

80 ML OLIVE OIL
2 TBSP BALSAMIC VINEGAR
I TSP MUSTARD POWDER
3 TSP CASTER SUGAR
2 TSP CHOPPED CORIANDER
LOTS OF FRESH BLACK PEPPER
TOASTED PUMPKIN SEEDS

METHOD

- Chop accordingly and toss the salad ingredients in a large bowl.
- Slice the biltong to 2-3mm slices.

  Note: you will need a very sharp knife to achieve this, please be careful!
- Add to the salad, the biltong and goat's cheese.
- Mix together the salad dressing ingredients, pour over salad (enough to taste) and sprinkle the toasted pumpkin seeds, just before serving, on top.

*Best to use fresh figs in season. Use pickled figs as a substitute if out of season.

GULP WINES RECOMMEND...

Julien Schaal Syrah

2011

THE CHICHESTER BILTONG COMPANY

South African founders of The Chichester Biltong Company, Simon and Monique, live in the UK on the glorious Sussex South Coast. They have been making Biltong for over 25 years, first in South Africa and now in the UK.

"We cycle down to the beautiful West Wittering beach, sit on the sand, drink beer and treat ourselves to my latest batch of wet, fatty Biltong... my favourite! Always spicy!" says Simon a self-confessed cycling fanatic. "However, Monique is a pain and always demands dry, non-fatty, thin-as-you-like, biltong! Talk about high maintenance!"

Pilates teacher Monique continues. "I am always on the go and I really need to up my protein intake. Biltong is the perfect source of low fat protein. I love to sip some South African Zalze wine and nibble some biltong. That's me... always making time for perfect moments that remind me of home!"

The beef used to make the biltong is sourced from Natural Farms Limited and The West Oxfordshire Meat Company. They only use the silverside of the beef to make their products.

"Here at The Chichester Biltong Company we have a commitment to quality. We believe in the highest standards for ourselves and for our products. That is why all the spices used, right down to the salt, are organic and sourced from EHL Finest Natural Ingredients and we only use distilled spirit vinegar from Good Food Wines Limited. The very best money can buy for us and for you!" says Simon. "No sugar, no preservatives, no MSG, no "E" numbers, no gluten."

www.biltongcompany.co.uk

PURE SPAIN

Pure Spain is a Spanish lifestyle company. They source authentic Spanish foods, fine wine, traditional Asturian Cider, a range of delightful olive wood products, traditional pottery, cookware and a very popular selection of toiletries for children and adults. Launched in 2007 the objective of the company, was to create a website selling Spanish products not readily available in the UK — to offer the British market a touch of authentic Spain.

Where possible the food products carry Denominación de Origen (Designation of Origin - DO). This is part of a regulatory classification system for Spanish wines (similar to the French appelations) but also for other foodstuffs like honey, meats and condiments. It guarantees regulation of quality and geographical origin among Spain's finest producers.

For the real Hispanophile, Pure Spain has sourced an exclusive range of whole legs of Jamon Iberico Bellota from a small producer in Salamanca. They are shipped direct to your door and can include a jamonero (a ham stand) and a special ham knife to carve. The Chorizo, Lomo and Salchichon come from the same producer to complete a stunning range of high quality acorn-fed charcuterie.

The Olive Jam and Almond Turron have both won Gold from the Great Taste Awards panel while many of the fine wines have won accolades – the Vizcarra Crianza 2010 has recently been awarded 94 points by leading US wine critic Robert Parker. Perhaps most impressive of all is the Manchego Gran Reserva from Dehesa de Los Llanos which was given the coveted title of "Best Cheese in the World' at the World Cheese Awards 2012.

As well as food, Pure Spain sell a range of authentic Spanish cookware and stunning hand painted Spanish ceramics.

www.purespain.co.uk

CHORIZO & SPROUTING BROCCOLI TORTILLA

PREP 20 **MINS**   **COOK** 30 **MINS**

INGREDIENTS (SERVES 2-4)

125 G PURE SPAIN
"CHORIZO IBERICO PICANTE"
125 G SPROUTING BROCCOLI
8 TBSP OLIVE OIL
1 GARLIC CLOVE
1 RED PEPPER, SLICED

1 GREEN PEPPER, SLICED
5 MEDIUM POTATOES,
PEELED & SLICED THINLY
2 ONIONS
6 LARGE FREE RANGE EGGS
1 SMALL JAR COUCHILLO OLIVES

METHOD

- Heat 1 tbsp. olive oil in a frying pan and cook the garlic, peppers and chorizo until the chorizo darkens.

- Heat another 6 tbsp. olive oil in a large frying pan and gently cook the onions until brown. Add the potatoes to this and cook for a further 30 minutes stirring often until they are cooked throughout.

- Pour off any excess oil then mix the potatoes and onions in a bowl with the chorizo and peppers, adding the pre-beaten eggs.

- Heat the frying pan once more with any remaining oil and add the egg mixture stirring regularly for about a minute. Let the tortilla settle, pushing all the vegetables down and cook until the underneath has gone a lovely golden brown.

- To turn the tortilla over, place a flat pan lid on top and carefully turn the frying pan upside down to transfer over to the lid. Then slide the tortilla back into the pan, ensuring that you keep as much as possible in place.

- Cook this until it matches the golden brown top. Then leave to cool before serving.

- Serve with black Spanish couchillo olives for that extra Mediterranean feel.

GULP WINES RECOMMEND...

Vina Palacega Rioja
2011

HOT SMOKED CHICKEN SALAD

PREP 30 **MINS**   **ASSEMBLY** 10 **MINS**

INGREDIENTS (SERVES4)

1 CHESIL SMOKERY "SMOKED
CHICKEN BREAST", SLICED
200 G SLICED GREEN CABBAGE
100 G MATCHSTICK CARROTS
100 G PEPPER

FOR THE DRESSING

20 ML SOY SAUCE
30 ML OLIVE OIL
20 ML HONEY
1 LIME
1 TSP CHOPPED CORIANDER

METHOD

- After chopping the vegetables mix them together in a large bowl.
- Keep the dressing really pure and literally mix together the olive oil, soy, lime juice, chopped coriander and honey. Pour the dressing on to the salad and toss the ingredients together.
- When plating up be careful to try not to get the chicken too immersed in the coleslaw and dressing, so that when you are eating you can still strongly taste the smokey flavour.

This recipe is almost like a dry coleslaw made wet with an Asian dressing.

GULP WINES RECOMMEND...

Santa Duc

2010

THE CHESIL SMOKERY

Chesil Smokery in West Dorset uses oak and apple wood from British trees, specially graded to produce the optimum size of tiny wood chippings that suit their wonderful old smoker. They source fresh fish from Samways, the famous fish merchants of Bridport and the best free-range chicken and poultry from Creedy Carver of Crediton, Devon.

Salmon, the one thing they can not source locally, comes from farms which are situated in areas of strong currents and big tides – this means they swim far more, producing a leaner and meaner texture and no oiliness in the fish. They won't sell smoked wild salmon – believing they are better off in rivers than being under pressure from commercial fishermen. They believe this this does not compromise their product. They have conducted taste tests and customers could not tell the difference between the Chesil Smokery standard product and wild. They will not sell smoked eel either as they are also under severe pressure in the wild too.

Chesil Smokery is an artisan smokehouse and their processes are, by and large, all by hand. Finely tuned judgment is frequently called upon to finesse cooking and curing times. They will not sell smoked products they have not smoked in their own kiln.

If you love smoked things like salmon, duck, venison - order some of this delicious smoked loveliness now!

www.chesilsmokery.com

BREAD À LA MER

Bread à la mer is a commercial Artisan bakery based in the cathedral city of Chichester, offering a unique product in West Sussex. They take inspiration from the area and its producers and as 'Real Bread' bakers they hand craft each loaf without the use of processing aids or artificial additives. Danny and his wife Katy started the business following Danny's career as a professional yacht skipper. After having their two sons he decided to concentrate on his other career as a chef to spend more time in the UK. He worked as a senior chef in many Sussex restaurants including the Goodwood Estate. They both felt there was a lack of fresh Artisan bread supplied to restaurants and so set up their own bakery, at first operating out of Katy's mothers kitchen in West Wittering, thus 'Bread by the Sea'! The business grew quickly and they now have a commercial bakery in Chichester where every morning they bake Pumpkin Seed & Walnut, Sussex Three Seed, Bavarian Sourdough, Spelt & Honey and Rye bread to name but a few.

"Our bread is created using traditional slow fermentation methods and naturally occurring 'wild yeasts' that go to make our range of Sourdough breads," explains Danny. This traditional style of bread making produces bread that is easier to digest and has a flavour far superior to other commercial bread. Bread a la Mer are passionate about using as many local products in their bread as possible including Wholemeal flour milled at the ancient working Lurgashall Water Mill at the Weald & Downland Open Air Museum in Singleton. Recently they have collaborated with the Gribble Inn micro brewery to produce a Sussex Beer Bread.

Bread à la Mer sell to award winning farm shops, delis, restaurants and a local estate. They regularly attend select shows throughout the year as well as local events such as The Garden Show, Weald & Downland events, The Rare Brand Markets, The Aldingbourne Trust events and the Pulborough Farmers' Market.

www.breadalamer.co.uk

VEGGIE BURGER ON WALNUT & PUMPKIN BREAD

PREP 40 **MINS**   **COOK** 10 **MINS**

INGREDIENTS (MAKES 6)

BREAD À LA MER "WALNUT
& PUMPKIN SEED" LOAF
2 CANS CANNELLINI WHITE BEANS
1 SWEET POTATO, MASHED
2 TSP MAPLE SYRUP
50 G WHOLEMEAL FLOUR

TO SERVE*

BAG OF PANKO BREADCRUMBS
VEGETABLE OIL
* SLICED AVOCADO
* LARGE SLICED TOMATO
* ROMAIN LETTUCE
* DIJON MUSTARD

METHOD

- Bake the sweet potato. You can either do this in the oven and then peel and mash, or an easier technique is to peel and slice the potato, place in a bowl covered in cling film, then microwave for 10 minutes. You should be able to mash it with a fork.

- Add the cannellini beans to the mash and mix. Squash in the seasoning, flour, salt and pepper to taste. It should be squishy and moist, but you should be able to make a patty. If not, add a few breadcrumbs or a little flour to thicken.

- Heat the vegetable oil in a pan. Form the mixture into burgers using your hands and cover with the panko breadcrumbs. Then fry off in the pan, you can do more than one for quickness. (You can also bake these if you wish, but if you choose to do this, only a little panko is needed).

- Once browned on both sides, place the burgers onto kitchen roll to drain excess oil.

- Serve on a thick slice of the Walnut loaf, serve with avocado, tomato, lettuce, mustard and plenty of seasoning.

GULP WINES RECOMMEND...

Pitchfork Shiraz
2009

Try seasoning with Lemon Pepper for extra flavouring!

GOAT'S CHEESE & TOMATO TART

PREP 20 **MINS**   **COOK** 25 **MINS**

INGREDIENTS (SERVES 2-4)

2 OZ CHEESEBOARD
"STAWLEY GOAT'S CHEESE"
200 G READYMADE
ALL-BUTTER PASTRY
I TBSP SOUR CREAM
I TSP GRAINY MUSTARD

2 LARGE LEEKS
I TBSP UNSALTED BUTTER
2 TSP FRESH THYME OR BASIL
200 G CHERRY
TOMATOES, HALVED

METHOD

- Pre-heat oven to 200°C / Fan 180°C / Gas 6.

- Flour your surface and then roll out the puff pastry into a rectangle (roughly the size you see in the picture). It's important to use the all-butter readymade pastry as it gives you a brilliant glaze from the butter on the tart, or if you have time make your own.

- In a bowl, mix together the sour cream, mustard and a little salt and pepper. Spread the mixture evenly across the pastry and fold over the edges (about ½ an inch). Pop this in the fridge for 10 minutes.

- Chop your leeks lengthwise, wash and slice fairly thinly. Melt the butter in a pan and add the leeks, stirring until soft for about 3 minutes. Then turn the heat down and continue to cook slowly as they caramelise.

- Arrange these over the other mixture on the pastry. Top this with the half sliced baby tomatoes and season.

- Bake this in the oven for 25 minutes, or until golden brown on the edges. After letting it cool briefly, add hand torn chunks of the goat's cheese and the chopped basil or thyme.

- If you would like the basil garnish, as per the recipe photo, then pinch the basil and chop as finely as you can.

GULP WINES RECOMMEND...

Sauvignon Touraine
2011 Buisee

THE CHEESEBOARD

THE CHEESEBOARD

Michael Jones bought The Cheeseboard in 1985 and has spent nearly 30 years scouting the world for stock. Although tiny in size, six customers is the maximum this independent cheese shop can accommodate, it is huge in its cheese offer.

Devoted cheese aficionados make the pilgrimage to the shop knowing the counter will be heaving with extraordinary cheeses. Michael is always on the hunt for anything exceptional that is worth a spot on the shelves of his shop. Each cheese selected is as indiviudal as its maker from Childwickbury, a lemony goat cheese made by Elizabeth Harris in St Albans to Coolea, a Gouda-style cheese made in Cork by Dutch couple Helene and Dick Willems.

In keeping with his commitment to ensuring his customers are knowledgeable about the best cheeses available in the UK and Europe, Michael has gone truly global. Cheeseboard is one of the few suppliers of handmade artisan cheeses from America. A firm favourite is Rogue River Blue, which is covered in Syrah grape leaves that have been soaked in homemade pear brandy, and matured for several months.

In 2011 The Cheeseboard launched a shopping website. Now cheese devotees can enjoy Michael's hand-picked cheeses much as those who make their weekly sojurn to the Greenwich shop.

www.cheese-board.co.uk

THE SHEFFIELD HONEY COMPANY

THE
SHEFFIELD HONEY
COMPANY

Jez Daughtry, who runs the Yorkshire based food producer, The Sheffield Honey Company, is putting his home town of Sheffield on the food heroes map. After being made redundant by computer firm IBM, Jez chose to become a full-time commercial bee farmer. Not an obvious career choice but Jez sees his bees as a true vocation rather than just work.

Beautifully fragrant, the blossom, soft set and heather honeys are all produced using the minimum amount of processing fuss and, therefore, are rich in natural enzymes and maintain their high pollen content.

However Jez is not content with just making delicious batches of honey from his 300 hives dotted around 30 city locations including rooftop apiaries. He is a revolutionist and is keen to create future generations of beekeepers in Britain. He runs the Urban Beekeeping Experience event, giving a practical introduction into the world of bees and beekeeping. He shows the various tasks a beginner beekeeper needs to master and the different types of hives he uses.

It is an intensive labour of love — sometimes he finds himself on a rooftop in the dead of night in 60-mile an hour winds strapping down his precious hives. Jez is truly passionate about his unique and genuine British food.

www.sheffield-honey.co.uk

FRUITY & NUTTY RICE SALAD WITH HONEY DRESSING

PREP 20 **MINS**   **COOK** 10 **MINS**

INGREDIENTS (SERVES 4)

400 G BASMATI RICE
1 TBSP TUMERIC
1 TBSP CUMIN
1 TSP CORIANDER
4 MEDIUM TOMATOES
¼ ONION

30 G PUMPKIN SEEDS
40 G SULTANAS
30 G LINSEEDS
30 G CRANBERRIES
4 SPRING ONIONS
3 TBSP GARLIC OIL

DRESSING

2 TSP RED WINE
VINEGAR
2 TBSP SHEFFIELD
"PURE BLOSSOM"
HONEY
2 TBSP LEMON JUICE

METHOD

- Cook the rice adding the turmeric, coriander and cumin to the water. Once cooked, leave to cool in an appropriate dish for serving.

- Dice the tomatoes and onion, and scatter over the rice adding the pumpkin seeds (toasted), sultanas, cranberries, linseeds (toasted) and spring onions.

- Make the dressing by combining the oil, vinegar, Pure Blossom honey and lemon juice and season. Pour this over the rice and mix everything all up together.

- Garnish with herbs if you wish.

We have found the bigger dish, the better, regarding presentation here...

GULP WINES RECOMMEND...

La Belle Pierre Rose
2011

BLACK TRUFFLE LASAGNE

METHOD

- Heat olive oil in a large pot with lid over a medium heat. Add the leeks and garlic, cook for a few minutes until soft. Add ½ of the mushrooms and brown off. Pour in red wine, cook until it almost disappears. Remove pot from heat. Mix the in sage, oregano, thyme and truffle. Season well.

- Put the milk and the bay leaf in another pan and heat gently — do not let the mixture boil. Remove bay leaf and leave to stand.

- Melt the butter in a saucepan then add the remaining mushrooms, until cooked. Stir in the flour mixture until blended. Gradually add the milk to this. Simmer for 10 minutes, or until it has really thickened. Add the nutmeg and season.

- Preheat oven to 180°C / Fan 160°C / Gas 4. Mix the ricotta, parsley, basil and lemon in a bowl. Thinly oil a baking dish. Add a thin layer of the milk mixture to the pan, then cover with a layer of lasagne sheets. Next is ½ of the mushrooms, then add ¼ of hand torn mozzarella and ¼ Parmesan. Cover this with another layer of lasagne sheets.

- Now place ½ the ricotta mixture over this. Add remaining mushrooms, another layer of lasagne, ¼ of the mozzarella and Parmesan. Next, place one last layer of lasagne and the rest of the ricotta. Spread the left over milk mixture over the top.

- Cover the dish with tin foil and bake in the oven for 30 minutes then increase the temperature to 230°C / Fan 210°C / Gas 8. Sprinkle the rest of the cheese on top, cook for another 10 minutes.

INGREDIENTS (SERVES 4)

2 TBSP TRUFFLE OIL
2 SLICED LEEKS
5 GARLIC CLOVES, SLICED
500 G MUSHROOMS - MIXED, YOUR CHOICE!
1 TBSP RED WINE
½ TBSP FRESH THYME
½ TBSP FRESH SAGE
½ TBSP DRIED OREGANO
½ FINELY SLICED BLACK TRUFFLE
(PLUS EXTRA LARGER SLICES FOR GARNISH)
½ PINT OF MILK
1 BAY LEAF
4 TBSP BUTTER
30 G FLOUR
PINCH GROUND NUTMEG
½ PACK OF RICOTTA
SMALL HANDFUL OF CHOPPED PARSLEY
½ LEMON ZEST
SMALL HANDFUL OF CHOPPED BASIL
100 G MOZZARELLA
100 G LASAGNE SHEETS
60 G GRATED PARMESAN

PREP 50 MINS   COOK 40 MINS

GULP WINES RECOMMEND...

Auramaris Vermentino

2011

serve with a drizzle of truffle oil if you have any,
if not then use your best Virgin olive oil...

FERNET-BRANCA
SPECIALTY OF
FRATELLI BRANCA of MILAN

APPETIZING
THE KING OF B

MISTER TRUFFLE

At the time Mister Truffle came to life, it was only possible to buy fresh truffles in wholesale quantities. So when Hugo Pickford-Wardle was unsuccessfully shopping for a small amount of fresh black winter truffle as a present for his dad he had the idea of a company that sold truffle by the gram.

Wholesale greengrocers Matt Smith and Paul Smith joined the team at their base at New Covent Garden Market and Mister Truffle was in business selling truffles worldwide to the worlds best restaurants and foodies alike. The company is based on three founding ideas - good ingredients should be accessible to everyone; haveing fun experimenting in the kitchen and food which should bring a smile to your face.

Truffle should not be seen as a forbidden fruit. With the proper know how a little truffle can go a very long way.

www.mistertruffle.com

ESPRESSO MUSHROOM COMPANY

Espresso Mushroom Company was founded by coffee-drinking, food-loving brothers Alex and Robbie, and friends Jon and Duncan. It is the ultimate fresh, home-grown and sustainable product.

The company, based in Brighton, collects over 4 tonnes of waste coffee grounds from local cafes. "Like us, the Oyster mushrooms love coffee! And they grow beautifully in the used coffee grounds," says Alex. "First we perfected growing fresh mushrooms to sell to top Brighton restaurants. The next step was to develop a simple and exciting kit to sell direct to the public so they could enjoy growing mushrooms at home."

The Kitchen Garden Mushroom Kit brings the excitement of growing your own food to life. After just one week, the mushrooms literally double in size every day! Nutritionally, Oyster Mushrooms are high in protein and fibre, low in calories and contain zero fat and cholesterol. They are fantastic to cook with and have a rich flavour with a fresh peppery scent.

Espresso Mushroom Company knows it is very important to reduce emissions and hopes their company plays a part in inspiring others to value resources and up-cycle other "waste" products too.

www.espressomushroom.co.uk

OYSTER MUSHROOM RISOTTO

PREP 10 **MINS**   COOK 40 MINS

INGREDIENTS (SERVES 2-4)

20 G OLIVE OIL
I ONION, CHOPPED
150 G RISOTTO RICE
420 ML OF STOCK
(USE VEGETABLE IF COOKING
FOR VEGETARIANS)

75 G ESPRESSO "OYSTER
MUSHROOMS", CHOPPED
20 G CHOPPED PARSLEY
35 G PARMESAN
I TBSP MASCARPONE

METHOD

- Place the onion and olive oil in a saucepan over a medium heat, and stir until softened. Then add your risotto rice and allow it to toast in the pan slightly, for a few minutes.

- Then gradually add the stock, bit by bit, stirring well as the rice is absorbing the liquid.

- After about 10 minutes, add the Espresso Oyster mushrooms and the remaining stock (still gradually).

- Once the rice is cooked, put the mascarpone, Parmesan and parsley into the pan and mix it in.

- Serve with extra gratings of Parmesan.

- For some children, you may want to finely chop the mushrooms.

GULP WINES RECOMMEND...
Auramaris Vermentino
2011

Get children into mushrooms early - grow the mushrooms with them!

LEMON INFUSED LAMB WITH APRICOT ISRAELI COUSCOUS

PREP 10 **MINS**   **COOK** 2 HOURS

INGREDIENTS (SERVES 8)

WELL HUNG "LAMB SHOULDER"
2 LEMONS (JUICE & GARNISH)
100 G ISRAELI COUSCOUS
2 TBSP LEMON JUICE
1 TSP BALSAMIC VINEGAR
2 TBSP OLIVE OIL

PINCH ALLSPICE & CAYENNE PEPPER
½ RED ONION CHOPPED
50 G TOASTED ALMONDS
1 CELERY STICK CHOPPED
6 DICED DRIED APRICOTS
HANDFUL OF CHOPPED PARSLEY

METHOD

- Pre-heat oven to 230°C / Fan 210°C / Gas 8.

- Rub the lamb with the lemon and squeeze it over it, covering it well. You can use preserved lemons here too if that is all you have. Put it in the oven for 30 minutes, then turn it down to 180°C / Fan 160°C / Gas 4. Cook for 30 minutes per pound.

- When you are almost ready to prepare the couscous to eat, add it to a saucepan with 1 tbsp. olive oil over a low heat. Cook this until it starts to brown. Add 180ml of boiling water, mix it up and cover with a lid. Let this cook through for 10 minutes.

- Once the couscous is cooked through (you may have to taste it to double check) take it off the heat and you shouldn't need to drain it, as the water should have been absorbed. Combine the remaining ingredients (except for the parsley) with the couscous and mix together thoroughly.

- Serve together with the cooked lemon and parsley to garnish.

GULP WINES RECOMMEND...

Parva Res Nero D'Avola

2011

THE WELL HUNG MEAT COMPANY

The Well Hung Meat Company is an organic meat company which has won stacks of awards. It all started about 10 years ago after farmer Geoff Sayers at Carswell Farm in Devon started selling organic beef and lamb to neighbours and friends. In 2001 he entered some products into the Soil Association Awards on a whim and was bowled over to receive a gong for his lamb in the blind tasting! He repeated his success and deciding two years in a row could not be put down to just luck The Well Hung Meat Company began.

In 2003, as demand for the meat grew, Geoff had to look beyond Carswell and started sourcing lamb and beef from other local organic farms. The following year, they employed a butcher and in 2005 he revved up The Well Hung Burger Van, travelling around the country to let people taste the advantages of organic meat. All the while new products were added to the range — bacon, mutton, sausages and venison.

Geoff developed a way to prepare the meat, so today all the butchery is done the traditional way by hand, with no machinery at all. There's something very unromantic about a buzz saw. As originators of the monthly meat box they also know a thing or two about selling online. All meat is cut fresh every week to order, vac-packed and delivered chilled not frozen. You can then decide what to do with it. It's fine in the fridge for a good few days — up to a week for most cuts, but slightly less for chicken and sausages. If you want to keep it for longer, pop it in the freezer and it'll keep there for up to six months. When it thaws out, it's as good as it was before you froze it, so freezing is an excellent way to store your meat.

The Well Hung Meat Company specialise in one thing — ensuring you get the freshest, highest quality, well hung, grass fed, organic meat for your table.

www.wellhungmeat.com

Photography: Rubies in the Rubble

INTERESTING VEGETABLES AND PLANTS

Balsamic & Honey Glazed Carrots
LUCY'S DRESSINGS

Braised Cabbage & Blackberry Vinegar
WOMERSLEY

Manchego Stuffed Chillies
MUSWELL HILL CHEESE SHOP

White Miso Aubergines
SOUS CHEF

Raw Tofu with Soya Sauce Dressing
CLEAN BEAN

Butternut Squash, Black Bean & Feta Tacos
THE GREEK DELI

Spiced Cauliflower with Garlic Pachadi, Dhal & Chapatis
MANJIRA

Green Bean Curry
BIT SPICY

Cretan Tomato & Zucchini Potato Gratin
MESTÓ ARTISAN OLIVE OIL

Freekeh Tabouleh
TERRA ROSSA

LUCY'S DRESSING

Lucy's Dressings is a classic kitchen table start-up business. Produced in Suffolk and originating from Lucy Mackenzie's very own kitchen, these home-made dressings are perfect to use on salads as well as pasta, meat or spread over toast. The Golden Dressing is inspired by the cold rapeseed oil produced locally at Hillfarm which has half the saturated fat of an olive oil based dressing.

Lucy developed the recipes to give food lovers a range of delicious dressings. "I've always found dressings available in the shops are over sweetened and over complicated," says Lucy. "So when I started creating my range I knew I had to use only the finest ingredients I could find."

The current range is five strong and includes a classic Balsamic; Zesty Mayo, Light Asian and French Bliss. While Lucy's Dressings could easily rescue any tomato or lettuce from obscurity they should not be relegated to the salad bowl.

These perfectly balanced dressings can be used as a marinade as well as to roast and fry. It is easy to see how this collection has made Lucy the winner of several Great Taste Awards.

www.lucysdressings.co.uk

BALSAMIC & HONEY GLAZED CARROTS

PREP 15 **MINS**   COOK 45 **MINS**

INGREDIENTS (SERVES 5)

5 ORGANIC CARROTS (AS THEY ALWAYS TASTE THE BEST)
100 G MUSCOVADO SUGAR
30 G MELTED BUTTER
2 TBSP LUCY'S "HONEY & BALSAMIC" DRESSING
30 G GOOD QUALITY, RUNNY HONEY

METHOD

- Peel the carrots and chop off any excess leaves, although we like to leave a little bit for decoration.

- Preheat oven to 180°C / Fan 160°C / Gas 4, and put the carrots into an ovenproof tray.

- Mix together the sugar, butter, Lucy's "Honey & Balsamic" dressing and honey into a bowl and then cover the carrots fully in the mixture, with a bit of seasoning.

- Cook these through for 45 minutes – or until you think they look done. Turn them during the cooking to ensure they are regularly covered in the marinade.

- Serve with a main dish, or as shown here with a side dip of honey and balsamic for that extra sweetness.

GULP WINES RECOMMEND...

Parva Res Cataratto
2011

BRAISED CABBAGE & BLACKBERRY VINEGAR

PREP 20 **MINS**   **COOK** 40 **MINS**

INGREDIENTS (SERVES 2-4)

25 G BUTTER
1 ONION, CHOPPED
500G RED CABBAGE, SLICED THINLY
2 TBSP MUSCOVADO SUGAR

2 TBSP WOMERSLEY "BLACKBERRY VINEGAR"
1 TSP POWDERED MIXED SPICES
150 ML APPLE JUICE
225 G BLACKBERRIES

METHOD

- Heat the butter in a pan and add the onion and cook through until soft. Add the red cabbage with the sugar, blackberry vinegar, spice and juice, and season.

- Cook this over a low heat for 30 minutes; occasionally stirring to ensure it is soft throughout.

- Add the blackberries and cook for a further 10 minutes.

- Serve with a main course, and try and plate with a pink dish as we have — for extra dramatic effect.

This dish great hot or cold - and especially one to two days old!

GULP WINES RECOMMEND...
Karl Johner Rivaner
2011

WOMERSLEY

WOMERSLEY
BOTANICALLY ENTHUSED

Forty years ago, for most of us, British vinegar had one use. It was simply a malt used as an accompaniment to a bag of chips. At Womersley Hall in Yorkshire, Martin Parsons and his wife Aline had very different ideas. Their son Rupert, who succeeded them at the reins of Womersley, explains, "My father Martin, who founded the company in 1979, wanted to have the intense, true and natural flavours from the fruit and herbs in our walled kitchen garden all year. He realised this could be done through a vinegar and he was keen to get across the idea that using spirit vinegar, one could harness the flavour of all these glorious British fruits and home grown herbs."

Over the years, Womersley have won numerous Taste Awards including a Top 50 Gold for their most popular Raspberry Vinegar and Gold for their Lime, Black Pepper & Lavender in 2012. The judges described them as "drop dead gorgeous vinegars!" They were amongst a small select group of Artisan food producers to supply the London Olympic Games.

When Rupert took over at Womersley, he was keen to rebrand the company to revitalize interest. His father was as colourful a character as the vinegars he created, so Rupert decided to make the designs reflect this with vibrant fruity colours which have great shelf appeal and look beautiful in any kitchen. Having won a grant through the Design Council, Rupert says "the process of rebranding was really invigorating as it made us look hard at what we do and where we wanted to go. We even have people buying our bottles now, just because they are so pretty."

Womersley are still proud to produce a stunning range using time-honoured methods and only natural ingredients. A little goes a long way with this astonishingly versatile ingredient, that can bring almost any recipe to life.

www.womersleyfoods.co.uk

MUSWELL HILL CHEESE SHOP

Cheeses of Muswell Hill is a 28 year old family run business that believes in high quality, handmade produce. They are a maturer, retailer, wholesaler and exporter of farmhouse and artisan cheeses. Champions of small dairies and producers ,Cheeses always try to buy direct. They stock over 230 different kinds of cheese, ranging from delicious farmhouse Montgomery cheddar to divine Pyrenean goat's cheese. The Cheeses shop is a tiny, beautiful jewel tucked away amongst the chic boutiques of Muswell Hill.

Their philosophy is simple. They would like everyone to love cheese as much as they do. The secret to achieving this is through sharing knowledge and enthusiasm with customers and introducing hand made cheeses to as many people as possible.

When it comes to caring for cheese they offer the following advice to keep it in peak condition as only a few have the luxury of a cellar or a larder so most customers use a fridge. Wrap the cheese in waxed paper and place a damp cloth over it to help it to contain its moisture. Keep it in the salad compartment of your fridge as this is less cold. When you are ready to eat your cheese take it out of the fridge a good hour before to let it warm to room temperature. Serve on a slate board, as the cheese looks great and stays cool, presenting it for eating in the optimum condition.

www.cheesesonline.co.uk

MANCHEGO STUFFED CHILLIES

(V)

PREP 20 **MINS**   **COOK** 10 **MINS**

INGREDIENTS (SERVES 4-8)

8 LONG CHILLIES (FIND THE BEST
ONES AT YOUR GREENGROCER!)
80 G MUSWELL LILL "MANCHEGO"
CHEESE, SLICED
90 G PLAIN FLOUR

60 G POTATO FLOUR
30 G BAKING POWDER
180 ML COLD WATER
SPRINKLING OF EXTRA FLOUR
PAN OF VEG OIL (FOR FRYING)

METHOD

- Cut the chillies length ways, and fill with the slices of cheese before closing them back up.

- Mix the two different flours in a bowl with the water.

- Half fill a small pan with oil and place over a high heat. Sprinkle the chillies with flour before coating with the tempura mix (all flours, baking powder and water mixed).

- Put them in the hot oil for roughly 2 minutes, or until crispy.

- Place them on kitchen roll to get rid of any excess oil.

- You can alter this recipe depending on your love for hot food. The further up you eat, the hotter the chilli gets as the seeds start to appear.

- If making for your children, get rid of the seeds in the first step, to create a much milder dish.

- Delicious served with soy sauce and sprinkled with good quality rock salt.

GULP WINES RECOMMEND...

Medievo Seleccion Especial
2010

WHITE MISO AUBERGINES

PREP 20 **MINS** **COOK** 25 **MINS**

INGREDIENTS (SERVES 1-2)

1 AUBERGINE, SLICED LENGTHWAYS
1 TBSP VEGETABLE OIL
25 G SOUS CHEF "WHITE MISO"
4 TSP FRESH GINGER, GREATED
2 TSP TOASTED SESAME OIL
1 TSP SOY SAUCE

1 TSP WHITE WINE VINEGAR
3 TSP TOASTED SESAME SEEDS
3 TBSP SPRING ONION,
FINELY CHOPPED

METHOD

- Preheat oven to 220°C / Fan 200°C / Gas 7. Brush both sides of the aubergine with the oil and place on baking parchment.

- Roast the aubergine for about 20 minutes, or until soft, turning once.

- Mix the white miso, ginger, sesame oil, soy sauce, vinegar in a bowl and whisk them together. Season to taste.

- Stir in half of the sesame seeds and half of the spring onion to the mix, and cover the aubergine with this.

- Place on a rack and cook for a further 5 minutes until brown around the edges.

- Take them out, and garnish with the remaining spring onion and sesame seeds.

GULP WINES RECOMMEND...

The Architect Chardonnay

2011

INTERESTING VEGETABLES AND PLANTS

101

SOUS CHEF

There is a world of flavour to explore at Sous Chef, the online destination for adventurous cooks, where you can find almost any ingredient. Sous Chef founder, Nicola Lando, trained in a Michelin star kitchen before opening her online store. On the site are hard-to-find ingredients normally sold in bulk, such as freeze-dried strawberries, aonori seaweed or hickory smoke powder, the world's hottest chilli, Raymond Blanc's favourite olive oil, a numbingly hot Sichuan pepper and a fruity acidic raspberry vinegar. They source with care from food producers who share a passion for flavour and quality. Their peppers, for example, come from a single harvest and region enabling you to enjoy the unique flavour of that terroir.

Based in London with a warehouse full of fabulous things, ready for next day delivery, Sous Chef has served over five thousand happy customers including some of the top restaurants in Europe since opening in 2012.

Why not infuse your dishes with aromatic cold smoke or try your hand at spherification with molecular ingredients? There are taste suggestions and cooking tips to help you improve your patisserie or sushi techniques and professional cookware and books to inspire your needs.

The team at Sous Chef have tasted their ingredients, tested their equipment, served guests with their tableware and cooked from their cookbooks — they believe they have the best job in the world!

www.souschef.co.uk

CLEAN BEAN

clean bean

Mapo doufu — pock-marked old woman's tofu — is the dish that got Neil McLennan hooked on tofu. He was living in Sichuan Province, China and eating this amazing tofu at the local snack bars. When he returned home to the UK, the tofu on offer was a big disappointment so he decided to make his own.

At Clean Bean making tofu is a craft. "In Asia, it is as appreciated as cheese production is in the UK," explains Neil. "The tofu I make is a combination of the very soft, silken variety that can be eaten raw in salads or soups and the firm variety that is used in cooking. The tofu I make is somewhere between the two."

All the tofu is completely handmade, a process of soaking the soya beans, cleaning them and cooking them. Then they are filtered to make a liquid which is set. Neil started with a stall at Spitalfields Organic Market, but to meet increasing demand he set up a workshop making tofu in the East End of London.

"When I started selling organic tofu 15 years ago, my customers were really surprised at how good it tasted," says Neil. "Tofu should be creamy-smooth in texture and have a clean, fresh, soya-bean taste. Most western producers are intent on getting rid of the inherent flavour — but it really should be recognised as an interesting ingredient in its own right."

www.cleanbean.co.uk

RAW TOFU WITH SOYA SAUCE DRESSING

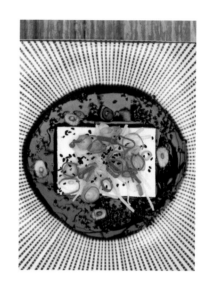

PREP 10 **MINS**   ASSEMBLY 5 MINS

INGREDIENTS   (SERVES 1-2)

½ PACK CLEAN BEAN "ORGANIC TOFU"
100 ML SOY SAUCE
2 FINELY CHOPPED SPRING ONIONS
SPRINKLING OF NIGELLA SEEDS
1 TSP CHOPPED GINGER
2 TSP CHOPPED CHIVES

METHOD

• Sit the tofu in the soy sauce, and then top with the rest of the ingredients.

This dish is supposed to be pure and simple, and all about the great quality tofu. Tofu should be eaten in a fuss-free way. In China, this is how they tofu.

GULP WINES RECOMMEND...
Chamonix Blanc
2011

BUTTERNUT SQUASH, BLACK BEAN & FETA TACOS

PREP 20 **MINS**   ASSEMBLY 10 MINS

INGREDIENTS (MAKES 4 TACOS)

½ BUTTERNUT SQUASH, CUBED & PRE-ROASTED
1 RED ONION, SLICED
150 G COOKED BLACK BEANS
HANDFUL OF CORIANDER
80 G GREEK DELI "FETA", CRUMBLED

1 CHILLI, THINLY SLICED DIAGONALLY - OR USE CHILLI FLAKES INSTEAD
4 SOFT WHITE TACOS - OR TORTILLA WRAPS
1 SMALL TUB SOUR CREAM

METHOD

- Place the sweet potato and black beans in a bowl and gently mix, making sure that the squash retains its shape.

- Load the mixture into the tacos.

- For best results – serve with sour cream.

GULP WINES RECOMMEND...

Calusari Pinot Grigio

2011

THE GREEK DELI

Travelling for years all around the Greek islands, Panos Maniotis and Clio Syrma discovered superb foods which excited them. Driven by this passion for the Greek gastronomy and a love for cooking they decided to establish a business in the UK and make the quality of Greek cuisine known to the British.

Greek food is part of the Mediterranean cuisine, the model of healthy eating consisting of ingredients such as extra virgin olive oil, olives, vegetables, rice, herbs, spices and fruit.

However, the difference between Greek and other Mediterranean foods is the oriental touch. Being at the crossroads between East and West, Greek cuisine has been influenced by Asia Minor and Middle East and this serves to make it more exciting and exotic.

It is also linked to holidays and good, relaxing times. Millions of British people travel to Greece every year and come back home looking for the tastes they have savoured. The Greek Deli supply authentic Greek ingredients to ensure you can make your Meze food the same way you had it on Crete or Rhodes - the perfect holiday souvenir.

Their range of premium products includes Extra Virgin Olive Oils, Pomace Oil, Vinegars, Premium Greek Olives, Greek Cheeses, Authentic Greek Yoghurt, Meze Food & Antipasti, Greek Pasta, Melina Tomato Sauces, Greek Pulses, Melina Ready Meals, Melina Dips, Greek Wines, Greek Lager, Ouzo & Tsipouro, Greek Sweets and Greek Honey.

www.thegreekdeli.com

MANJIRA

manjira

As owners of an established frozen, ready-meal company, Savithri and Gerry Newell set themselves a new challenge. They wanted to bring the true taste of Savithri's home city of Hyderabad in Southern India to the UK. Pachadis refers to a traditional South Indian side-dish, broadly translated as a food which has been pounded.

Using her mother's original recipes Savithri created Manjira Pachadis. Made using the typical ingredients of her birthplace these authentic south Indian chutneys are unlike their European derivatives. They are made without sugar or vinegar and are gluten free.

There are several Pachadis in the range including garlic, tomato, onion, tamarind and ginger. As they are oil based they can be used like a pesto sauce, stirred directly into cooked pasta, rice or mashed potatoes. They can be eaten as a chutney with Indian food and they are also delicious with cheese and in sandwiches. Manjira are unique in producing a range of Pachadis in the UK.

www.manjira.com

SPICED CAULIFLOWER WITH GARLIC PACHADI & DHAL

PREP 15 **MINS**   COOK 20 MINS

INGREDIENTS (SERVES 2-4)

200 G CAULIFLOWER
25 ML OLIVE OIL
1 TSP CHOPPED CORIANDER
1 TSP CUMIN
1 TSP NIGELLA SEEDS
1 TSP TURMERIC

2 PRESSED CLOVES OF GARLIC
5 CHAPATIS
LENTIL DHAL
RAITA
MANJIRA'S "GARLIC PACHADI"

METHOD

- Preheat oven to 180°C / Fan 160°C / Gas 4.
- Combine the olive oil, coriander, cumin, Nigella seeds, turmeric and garlic in a bowl.
- Add the cauliflower and coat generously.
- Spread evenly into a baking tray, and bake in the oven for 20 minutes, until soft.
- Serve with chapatis, garlic pachadi, dhal and a mint raita dip.

You can get lentil dhal from your local Indian restaurant or just buy it readymade but online, there are many, many versions of dhal to choose from.

GULP WINES RECOMMEND...

Karl Johner Rivaner
2011

GREEN BEAN CURRY

PREP 15 **MINS**   **COOK** 25 **MINS**

INGREDIENTS (SERVES 2)

2 TBSP VEGETABLE OIL
5 WHOLE CLOVES
1 ONION, SLICED
2 TSP SUGAR
1 TOMATO, CHOPPED
½ RED PEPPER, SLICED

BIT SPICY "SULAWESI" CURRY MIX
200 G GREEN BEANS,
TRIMMED & HALVED
300 ML VEGETABLE STOCK

METHOD

- Heat the oil in a saucepan and add half of spice mix. Heat through, then add the onion and sugar, and cook until the onions soften.

- Add the pepper, tomato and stock and cover with a lid, leaving to simmer for 10 minutes, this is now your base curry sauce.

- Add 3/4 of the beans, blanch them in the curry sauce so that they are still a vibrant green for decoration purposes but tender to eat. This should take another 10 minutes.

- The remains of the beans, blanch in hot water for 10 minutes for decoration.

- Season to taste, then pile on a plate with the beautiful green beans on top.

- Serve with boiled or basmati rice.

GULP WINES RECOMMEND...
Parva Res Cataratto
2011

Why would you need meat with a curry this good!

BIT SPICY

Bit Spicy was founded after an evening of eating. Founders Andrew and Liz Anderson had cooked their socks off — chicken vindaloo, venison rendang, keema peas, chickpea and potato curry, a dhal — for a most appreciative audience. Everyone they knew enjoyed eating curry but it hit them — none of their friends ever made it. They were the only people who actually cooked a curry from scratch — dry-roasting their own spices, growing and grinding the chillies and making their own spice blends.

Bit Spicy grew from the realisation that many curry cook books are overcomplicated and inaccurate. The couple wanted to share the secret of making restaurant style curry at home and created a range of Indonesian, Malaysian, Indian and Mexican spices to be cooked at home by enthusiastic curry amateurs. Every single recipe has been road-tested by friends and family for their flavour and ease of preparation. And finally, Bit Spicy gives you a secret sauce recipe — a simple concoction of onion, garlic and ginger providing the foundation for most curry dishes as well as a wide selection of free recipes on their website.

www.bitspicy.com

MESTÓ ARTISAN OLIVE OIL

Crete in Greece is famous for its ancient olive trees and stunning Extra Virgin Olive Oil. On the southern side of the island, in the shadows of Mt Ida, the trees of Mestó grow under the Mediterranean sun. "Our oil comes from my family's trees — some I planted with my Father and Grandfather when I was small, others have been standing for generations." says Vasilis, owner of Mestó Artisan Olive Oil. "Now it is our turn to take care of, and replenish the land and trees."

Vasilis is born and bred Cretan and always harboured the dream of rebuilding his Papou's house and tending the trees he had grown up with. Now every winter from November to February, together with his English partner, Cate, Vasilis coaxes the olives from their trees, harvesting come snow or shine but never in the rain. He explains, "we look forward to the rainy days because no work can be done so we make a big fire and cook up a feast."

Mestó is single estate premium Extra Virgin Olive Oil made from a single variety of olive — the very Greek Koroneiki with its distinctive golden green colour, robust and fruity flavour which produce a grassy nose and peppery tickle.

Vasilis reiterates, "our oil comes from our trees and only our trees. It isn't blended with Yiani's from down the street nor from the co-op, just our trees. Between us we have nurtured and harvested every olive that has gone into making our beautiful oil. We have watched them grow." Once harvested the olives are taken to the local mill, run by old school friends Manolis and Michaelis, where it is pressed and left to rest and settle for a couple of months, before being put into tins and sent on its way by road to the UK.

Cate and Vasilis believe farmers are the custodians of the earth and have a responsibility to work consciously and sustainably, mindful of what is being passed on and of the footprint that's left. Gentle cultivation, for the birds and the bees, the flowers and the trees, for the good of the oil and the good of the soil.

www.mesto.co.uk

CRETAN TOMATO & ZUCCHINI POTATO GRATIN

PREP 1 HOUR

INGREDIENTS (SERVES 4)

500 G RICOTTA CHEESE
400 G FETA
300 G POTATOES, THINLY SLICED
700 G COURGETTE, THINLY SLICED
5 MEDIUM TOMATOES, THINLY SLICED
3 TBSP MINT, FINELY CHOPPED
6 TBSP MESTÓ ARTISAN "EXTRA
VIRGIN" OLIVE OIL & EXTRA TO DRIZZLE

METHOD

- Preheat oven to 180°C / Fan 160°C / Gas 4. Grease your oven dish.

- Mix the cheeses together in a bowl and season. Do the same with the potatoes in a separate bowl and add 2 tbsp. olive oil.

- In your dish, layer 1/3 of the potatoes neatly and season. Now do the same with 1/3 of the courgettes (sliced lengthways) and season. Add 2 tbsp. olive oil. Add 1/3 of the cheeses and spread evenly. It is now that you add the chopped mint.

- Repeat the process again, twice. Now layer with sliced tomatoes (leaving 4 slices for garnish, as shown in the picture), add the last 2 tbsp. olive oil and pop your tomato garnish on top.

- Cover your dish with tin foil and bake for 1 hour. Then remove the foil and put back in the oven for another 30 minutes – until the potatoes are soft. Let it sit for a few minutes, then serve warm with a drizzle of olive oil.

GULP WINES RECOMMEND...

Parva Res Cataratto
2011

FREEKEH TABOULEH

PREP 45 **MINS**   **COOK** 35 **MINS**

INGREDIENTS (SERVES 2)

100 G TERRA ROSSA FREEKEH
50 ML TERRA ROSSA GARLIC OIL
PINCH OF TERRA ROSSA DUKKA
1 TBSP PARSLEY, CHOPPED
1 TBSP MINT, CHOPPED
½ CUCUMBER, DICED

FOR THE DRESSING*

150 G BABY TOMATOES
1 POMEGRANATE (SEEDS)
1 LEMON
* JUICE OF 1 LEMON
* ½ TSP ALL SPICE
* ½ TSP CINNAMON

METHOD

- Soak the Freekeh in cold water and wash, making sure there are no stones. Drain away all excess water. Put a dash of the garlic oil in a pan and fry off the Freekeh.

- Add the Dukka and season. Cover with boiling water, roughly 1 cm above the Freekeh and boil for 3 minutes. Then reduce the heat, cover with a lid and leave alone to simmer for 30 minutes (without disturbing the mix).

- Mix together the rest of the garlic oil with the juice of the lemon, allspice and cinnamon.

- Mix all contents together, minus the pomegranate. Plate up and scatter the pomegranate seeds on top. For the ripped lemon effect that you see in our picture, slice an inch of the lemon with a knife, then put your thumbs in and rip apart.

There are numerous versions of a recipe method for a Tabouleh. Please note, this is not a traditional Arabian version, this is our chef's personal one.
To get an Arabian method, please visit Terra Rossa online.

GULP WINES RECOMMEND...

Calusari Pinot Grigio
2011

TERRA ROSSA

TERRA
ROSSA
Exquisite Arabian
Specialities
www.terra-rossa.com

In 2005, Iraqi-born British Palestinian, Hanan Samara, who is passionate about Middle-Eastern cuisine, opened the doors of Terra Rossa to introduce the delicious and mostly unexplored flavours of the Levant to the UK.

Terra Rossa started by importing Zait & Zaatar — Arabic for Sinolea olive oil and thyme mix — essentially a Mezza appetiser and often the first meal of the day. Sinolea is Terra Rossa's premium Jordanian cold-dripped extra virgin olive oil made from hand-picked, stone crushed, half green olives. It is traditionally eaten with Zaatar, sesame seeds and sumac. Together they form the main ingredient for making Manakeesh — the ubiquitous Levant Pizza.

Fast forward eight years and Terra Rossa's range has won multiple food awards in the UK and abroad. Its product offering has grown to include five infused extra virgin olive oils, Dukka Coriander and Sumac herb mixes, an Arabian range of pomegranate molasses, date molasses and rose and orange blossom waters. The tempting Anglo-Arabian sauces and dips are Dukka Harrisa, Baba's Rashi & Dibis, Aubergine and Tomato relishes and exotic Fiery Zhoug.

The new must-have ingredient is Freekeh. An early harvest green wheat that is extremely nutritious and an incredibly versatile grain to cook with. A favourite recipe is to cook Freekeh, with the Dukka Coriander mix, Olive Oil infused with Garlic served with Harissa, Fattoush salad dressed with Olive Oil infused with Lemon, Sumac dressing and a Greek Style yoghurt and cucumber dip on the side.

Great Taste Award winning ranges are perfect as foodie gifts and are beautifully presented with hand-painted dipping bowls or hampers.

www.terra-rossa.com

INTERESTING VEGETABLES AND PLANTS

PUDDINGS

Raw Chocolate & Orange Upside Down Cake
THE RAW CHOCOLATE CO.

British Summer Fruit Pudding
YARTY CORDIALS

Blueberry, Blackberry & Passion Fruit Pavlova
MRS DARLINGTON & DAUGHTERS

Lemon Cheesecake with Chocolate Biscotti Crust
PEACE OF CAKE LONDON

Matcha & Vanilla Cream Cake
THE TEA STUDIO

Beetroot, Ginger & Apple Summer Crumble
JUST INGREDIENTS

Raspberry, Fig, Pecan & Ginger Ice Cream Cake
CAROLINE'S DAIRY

Lemon & Berry Tart
ROSEBUD PRESERVES

Sticky Date Madeleines with Butterscotch Sauce
THE FUDGE KITCHEN

Granola — Knickerbocker Glory Style
SCRUMSHUS

THE RAW CHOCOLATE COMPANY

Established in 2006, the raw chocolate company is a hit all over the world. Their range includes silky smooth raw chocolate bars in two sizes and the unique, multi-award nominated raw chocolate covered mulberries, goji berries and raisins. They also produce raw supreme foods — such as cacao products, natural sweeteners, berries and seeds — giving you the freedom to come up with your own sublime creations.

All the products are vegan, most are Fairtrade and organic and the factory is solar and wind powered in the hills behind Brighton, West Sussex. They lovingly create the raw chocolate and raw chocolate berries in small batches and take extreme care to bring you the very best chocolate experience they can. They pick only the finest ingredients, spend longer than most manufacturers grinding and blending them to give the smoothest, most intense raw chocolate experience. Through all this they maintain temperatures below 42°C to retain as many nutrients as possible.

"Chocolate makes us happy," says choco wizard in charge, Linus. "And we make the chocolate happy too, making sure we are in the right mood when we go to work. We hope you enjoy our passion."

www.therawchocolatecompany.com

RAW CHOCOLATE & ORANGE UPSIDE DOWN CAKE

PREP 30 **MINS**   **COOK** 1 **HR** 30 **MINS**

INGREDIENTS (SERVES 4-6)

2 TBSP OLIVE OIL
350 G "COCONUT PALM SUGAR"
3 TBSP CHOPPED CRYSTALLISED GINGER
800 G FLOUR
2 RIPE ORANGES
WALNUTS, ROUGHLY CHOPPED
2 TSP BAKING POWDER
1 TSP BAKING SODA
1 ½ TSP GROUND GINGER
1 TSP GROUND CINNAMON
½ TSP SALT
PINCH OF ALL SPICE
2 EGGS
175 G DARK MOLASSES
2 TBSP "RAW CACAO POWDER"
300 ML BUTTERMILK
1 TUB CLOTTED CREAM, TO SERVE

METHOD

- Preheat oven to 150°C / Fan 130°C / Gas 2.

- Grease your cake tin and line with greaseproof paper. Spread 2 tbsp. butter on base and sprinkle with 100g of the coconut palm sugar and crystallised ginger.

- Peel and slice the oranges so that they look like the circular formula as shown in our picture, about ½ inch thick. Layer these, and the walnuts, in the pan.

- Mix together the flour, raw cacao powder, baking powder, baking soda, ginger, cinnamon and all spice.

- In another bowl, quickly whisk the rest of the butter and sugar, before slowly adding the eggs. Now add the molasses, the flour mixture and buttermilk, and carry on beating quickly until it has formed a nice smooth mix. Pour this over the oranges.

- Put the cake in the oven for an hour and a half, and check that it is cooked through before removing. Leave to cool before removing. Serve with clotted cream.

GULP WINES RECOMMEND...

The Stump Jump
2010

BRITISH SUMMER FRUIT PUDDING

PREP 45 **MINS**   COOK 15 MINS

INGREDIENTS

100 ML YARTY "RASPBERRY & ELDERFLOWER" CORDIAL
50 G CASTER SUGAR
1 KG FRESH SUMMER FRUITS, MIXED
MEDIUM WHITE BREAD, SLICED (8 REQUIRED)

METHOD

- Wash the fruit, and slice the larger pieces. Put them in a pan with the sugar and the Raspberry & Elderflower cordial, over a low heat, stirring well.

- Sieve fruit mix into another bowl, pushing down lightly on the fruits with a spoon to extract juices. Keep the fruit and juice mix.

- Line a rounded pudding bowl with cling film, make sure that the edges hang out.

- De-crust your bread slices. Dip each slice in the juices and then line the bowl carefully, ensuring that there are no gaps in between. Look at our picture for pattern inspiration. Get rid of any excess bread that sticks out of the top with some scissors.

- Pour the fruit mix into the bowl to the top. Then place the last slices of soaked bread on top to fill in the gaps.

- Wrap hanging cling film over the pudding tightly, place a plate on top that fits in well. Weigh down with anything you have, we used 2 cans of beans. Put in fridge overnight.

- When ready to serve, take off weights and undo the cling film. Once you have decided on a serving dish, put in place and slowly turn over the pudding by putting the dish on a plate and turning it over.

- Carefully take off the bowl and extra cling film, pour over any of the juices you have left and serve with or without cream.

GULP WINES RECOMMEND...

Champagne Louis Brochet

YARTY CORDIALS

YARTY

Yarty is Britain's premium artisan cordial handmade in Hampshire to old family recipes without any nasty added extras. The company originally made Scotch Eggs to supply to local pubs. To comply with food regulations they had to be registered as a food producer with South Somerset Council. On a visit the inspector was offered a glass of their homemade cordial and said they should forget about the eggs and sell the cordial instead!

Yarty's owner Jayne has been making cordials using recipes from her Grandmother Mabel who used cordials to cook. This was years before fridges and a cordial was one of the only ways to preserve the fruit. Through trial and experience Jayne now uses fruits and herbs traditionally grown in Britain, along with citrus fruits, sugar and spring water to give a clean taste which customers love.

"We have developed a special method of gentle pasteurisation, which enables us to create our cordials without the addition of any artificial preservatives." explains Jayne. They use real fruit for all of the cordials so the colours alter as the seasons change and different fruits become available - one sip and you can tell that it is not mass produced.

"We ride with the natural seasons that occur during the year, accepting changes in the produce and adapting the recipe preparation to maintain overall quality," says Jayne. "You will not find any of our wonderful range of handmade fruit cordials and vinegars in any supermarkets. We leave that to others. Yarty is the covert cordial, for those of a more discerning nature. 'England in a bottle' according to Hollywood actor Johnny Depp.

www.yartycordials.co.uk

MRS DARLINGTON & DAUGHTERS

Mrs Darlington's

Mrs Darlington's is a well-established family run business in Cheshire which has been making its range of over seventy award-winning curds, jams, marmalades, chutneys and sauces for thirty years. Mrs Darlington is still at the helm and her aim remains the same as it ever was — to craft delicious products with a truly homemade taste.

This Cheshire success story started back in 1981 when the Darlington family found themselves with a surplus of eggs from the family farm. Not wishing them to go to waste, Mrs Darlington decided to use the eggs to make a batch of her family's favourite lemon curd and sold it to local shops. Over the following months requests started pouring in from customers asking if Mrs Darlington would consider selling her other homemade jams, chutneys, marmalades and sauces too. Soon the farmhouse was just too small and in 1985 farm buildings were converted into a new kitchen. Ladies from the local village were drafted in to help and Mrs Darlington's daughter Sarah joined the team. Since then Mrs Darlington's has just kept growing, relocating to even bigger premises in 1992 and Sarah's sister, Wendy, joined the family team too.

Today, Mrs Darlington's remains a family concern. Following in Mrs Darlington's innovative footsteps, Sarah has her own range of tasty mustards, table sauces and pickles and Wendy has a delicious range of cooking sauces.

www.mrsdarlingtons.com

BLUEBERRY, BLACKBERRY & PASSION FRUIT PAVLOVA

PREP 40 **MINS**   **COOK** 15 **MINS**

INGREDIENTS (SERVES 4-6)

200ML MRS DARLINGTON
& DAUGHTERS
"PASSIONFRUIT CURD"
4 EGG WHITES
350G CASTER SUGAR

I TSP CORNFLOUR
I TSP WHITE WINE VINEGAR
600 ML DOUBLE CREAM
HANDFUL OF BLUEBERRIES
I PASSION FRUIT

METHOD

- Preheat the oven to 150°C / Fan 130°C / Gas 2.

- Whisk the egg whites until fluffy. Then slowly add the caster sugar until you reach a stiff meringue mixture. Gently stir in the cornflour and vinegar. Alternatively, use your own faithful meringue recipe if you prefer.

- Line a baking tray with baking paper. Then spoon round blobs of mixture next to each other so that they join up to form a circle. Make a slight dip to make room for the filling in the middle.

- Put in the oven for 50 minutes and then turn off the oven leaving the meringue to cool inside.

- To serve, peel the meringue gently from the baking paper. Whip the cream and spread on the meringue. Then top with passionfruit curd and garnish with blueberries and passionfruit seeds.

- For a slightly healthier alternative, the dish also tastes excellent with natural yoghurt or even crème fraiche.

GULP WINES RECOMMEND...

Prosecco Dolci Colline

LEMON CHEESECAKE WITH CHOCOLATE BISCOTTI CRUST

PREP 2 HRS 30 MINS   **COOK** 15 MINS

INGREDIENTS (SERVES 4-6)

2 PACKS PEACE OF CAKE
"CHOCOLATE BISCOTTI"*
125 G BUTTER
300 G MASCARPONE CHEESE
200 G ICING SUGAR
400 G CREAM CHEESE

4 LEMONS
200 G GRANULATED SUGAR
1 TSP ARROW ROOT

*DAIRY, WHEAT, GLUTEN &
 CASEIN FREE BISCOTTI, WOW!

METHOD

- Line an 8 inch flan tin with cling film. Bash up the biscotti (either with a pestle and mortar or with a rolling pin and strong plastic food bag) until they are quite fine. Place in the bottom of the tin. Melt 75g of the butter and pour it over the biscotti, forming a base for your cheesecake. Allow to set in the fridge for 1 hour.

- Whilst this is setting, combine the cheeses and icing sugar in a bowl. When ready, place this evenly on top of the biscotti base. Allow this to set for another hour in the fridge.

- To create 4 glazed lemon pieces, slice them very thinly and cook them in a pan over a gentle heat with the remaining butter and 100g sugar. Cook these very gently until they look glazed. Set aside to cool.

- For the lemon glaze on top of the cheesecake filling, mix the remaining lemon juice, 100g sugar and arrow root in another bowl, gently heat the liquid then let cool. When cooled, pour on top of the filling. To set the glaze, place in fridge for 10-15 minutes.

GULP WINES RECOMMEND...

The Stump Jump
2010

You could choose dairy free cheese and butter if you prefer...

PEACE OF CAKE LONDON

Peace of Cake London are a godsend for those inflicted with food intolerance. They bake their gluten and dairy free cakes from scratch so if you are following a gluten/wheat-free and dairy-free/casein-free (GFCF) diet then this is the perfect place for you to find a sweet treat. Peace of Cake London offer a range of everyday cakes and biscuits such as shortbread and brownies and a bespoke celebration range too. The thought of gluten and dairy free baking might not appeal to those who do not suffer any intolerances but these cakes have everyone scrambling for a larger slice. Their blueberry muffin won a gold star at the prestigious Great Taste Awards too.

They always use caster sugar, avoiding low calorie sweeteners on principle, and because they bake from scratch they can easily make a cake using fructose instead of sugar upon request, so cakes are suitable for diabetics as well! They also offer sugar-alternative (xylitol or stevia) options for some of their most popular products, so hopefully even more of you can enjoy a special treat.

Some of the most frequent queries are to do with the main ingredients. Almost all of the cakes and biscuits have a base mix which includes a free from gluten and wheat flour blend (rice, potato, tapioca, maize, buckwheat). They use free range eggs and a dairy free spread which is made of sunflower and other vegetable oils, raising agents (mon calcium phosphate, sodium bicarbonate), Xanthan Gum, salt, emulsifier and colour (natural carotenes). To the base they may add, where necessary, nuts, fruit, lactose free chocolate chips and other natural flavours.

www.peaceofcakelondon.co.uk

TEA STUDIO

TEA STUDIO

High in the Himalayan foothills of northern India, Hannah Scott and business partner, David Balfour, decided to start a tea business. Tea Studio, an independent company selling high quality loose leaf teas, tisanes and teaware, launched as an online retailer in 2012.

David and Hannah believe the personal connection with all their producers is crucial and their goal is to be able to visit and work directly with all of the estates whose tea they sell. The story behind each tea is key to standing out from the crowd. Each tea on the site is given an interesting biography. The aristocratic Ceylon Kenilworth — a single estate black tea from the 700-acre estate in Sri Lanka named after the English Castle. The Jasmine Pearls — an exceptional loose leaf tea, where the skillfully hand rolled pearls of green tea are scented with thousands of freshly picked jasmine blossoms whose heavenly and exotic perfume is slowly absorbed by the tea.

Along with tea, David and Hannah's passion for art has led them down a very creative path for the brand. Each tea is represented by a different artist's work on the packaging and a local potter has designed their current teaware range.

The company has a selection of 25 teas from around the world and is now expanding to offer their products to shops, cafés, restaurants, pubs, hotels and businesses.

www.teastudio.co.uk

MATCHA & VANILLA CREAM CAKE

PREP 1 **HOUR**   **COOK** 45 **MINS**

INGREDIENTS (SERVES 6-8)

480 G FLOUR
3 TBSP TEA STUDIO
"MATCHA" POWDER
2 TSP BAKING POWDER
140 G UNSALTED
BUTTER

300 G CASTER SUGAR
4 EGGS
1 VANILLA POD
½ TSP VANILLA EXTRACT
175 ML COCONUT MILK
PINCH OF SALT

FOR THE ICING

30 G UNSALTED BUTTER
220 G ICING SUGAR
8 TBSP COCONUT MILK
2 TSP VANILLA ESSENCE
"GYOKURO" LEAVES,
TO DECORATE

METHOD

- Preheat oven to 180°C / Fan 160°C / Gas 4. Grease or line two 20cm cake tins. Dust with flour, and set aside.

- Sift together the flour, baking powder, salt and matcha powder.

- In a different bowl, whiz the butter, sugar, and gradually the eggs for a few minutes until looking like a normal cake mixture. Scrape the pods for the beans and extract into this and mix in.

- Slowly add the flour mixture, turning and folding with your spoon or spatula bit by bit. In between adding the flour, pour small quantities of the coconut milk in as well. Eventually it should look lovely and smooth.

- Pour half of the cake mix into each tin, and put in the oven for 25–30 minutes, or until done.

- Let the cake cool, and mix together your icing ingredients. Evenly spread over the cake once cool. Sprinkle with Tea Studio "Gyokuro" tea leaves for decoration.

GULP WINES RECOMMEND...

Puy de Dome
2010

Please note how fantastically long Tea studio's Gyokura leaves are for the decoration!

BEETROOT, GINGER & APPLE SUMMER CRUMBLE

PREP 40 **MINS**   COOK 30 **MINS**

INGREDIENTS (SERVES 4)

700 G COOKING APPLES, PEELED & CHOPPED

1 PK COOKED BEETROOT, CHOPPED

50 G BUTTER (FOR THE CRUMBLE)

100 G GRANULATED SUGAR

50 G FLOUR

50 G SUGAR

30 G BUTTER (FILLING)

300 ML APPLE JUICE

75 G CASTER SUGAR

1 TBSP GINGER OIL

50 G CUT GINGER

METHOD

- Place the apples and the caster sugar in a pan over a low heat and cook until they are soft, but not overcooked. Take of the heat and set aside.

- Put the beetroot in another pan and add the rest of the sugar, 30g butter and the apple juice and Just Ingredients "Ginger Oil" and cook gently until the liquid has turned into a sweet glaze.

- Make the crumble topping by rubbing the flour, 50g butter and granulated sugar together.

- Place the apples and beetroot in an oven proof dish and cover with the crumble topping. Sprinkle Just Ingredients "Cut Ginger" over the top.

- Bake for 30 minutes until golden brown.

GULP WINES RECOMMEND...

The Stump Jump

2010

Don't pigeon hole beetroot!

JUST INGREDIENTS

JustIngredients
QUALITY INGREDIENTS DIRECT TO YOUR DOOR

Passionate about culinary and botanical ingredients, the Just Ingredients company seek out the best herbs and spices from the top producers around the world. They only source the highest standard of products and by purchasing from source, they can pass these savings on to their customers.

They have one of the largest ranges of ingredients online. Much more comprehensive than you will find on the high street or in your local supermarket. From turmeric to oregano, carob to ashwagandha. They also stock other herbs, spices, powders, oils and tinctures. The product range is exciting and diverse and when using their quick search button online customers are sure to come across some interesting finds.

Their customers include restaurants and chefs, health food shops, sandwich shops, market traders, sausage manufacturers, seasoning blenders and many individuals households. So if you want to make a huge Christmas cake for your family we can sell you dark muscovado sugar in a 25kg bag!

A young and vibrant business they aim to provide the UK and European markets with quality raw ingredients direct to your door. All of their products are non-irradiated and GMO free. They also supply a number of products suitable for vegan, vegetarian, nut-free and wheat-free diets.

www.justingredients.co.uk

CAROLINE'S DAIRY

A small family business run by Caroline and Chris Spiby, on Chalder Farm in Sidlesham. Caroline's Dairy uses fresh milk from their own mixed breed dairy herd to produce luxury ice cream. Their secret is happy cows, producing better creamier milk which makes Caroline's ice cream taste like no other.

Chris runs the dairy with a milking herd of 500 mixed bred cattle. Most of the fields where the cows graze are water meadows which form part of the RSPB Pagham Harbour Nature Reserve. Conservation is a very important part of the farm which provides an ideal habitat for wild animals, birds and insects which the Spiby's are keen to preserve for future generations.

Wide field margins are left uncultivated and are used as hunting corridors by Barn Owls and for nesting by Skylarks, Yellowhammers and English Partridge. Water voles have become re-established along the many watercourses and Brown Hares can also be seen racing and boxing in the spring when they are known as "Mad March Hares"!

As the business has grown Caroline has supported other local businesses, always sourcing as locally as possible. She employs mums from her village of Sidlesham known affectionately as "The Happy Cows." The mums work closely together supporting one another with work and childcare - there are times when all their children are playing in Chalder Farm garden, whilst their Mums are working hard making the ice cream.

"I hope you enjoy eating our ice cream as much as we enjoy making it." says Caroline Spiby, farmer's wife, mother and artisan ice cream maker.

www.carolinesdairy.co.uk

RASPBERRY, FIG, PECAN & GINGER ICE CREAM CAKE

PREP 24 HOURS   **ASSEMBLY** 20 MINS

INGREDIENTS (SERVES 4-6)

500 G RASPBERRIES
2 LITRES OF CAROLINE'S DAIRY "HONEY & GINGER" ICE CREAM
500 ML RASPBERRY COULIS (CAN USE JAM WITHOUT PIPS)
3 CRUNCHIE BARS, CHOCOLATE REMOVED (HONEYCOMB)
I TBSP CRUSHED HAZELNUTS
I TBSP PECANS

METHOD

- Line loaf tin (as shown on the previous page) with baking paper.
- Spoon the ice cream in a large bowl and leave to soften. Add the raspberries, hazelnuts, pecans and the coulis and gently mix together to create a swirly effect.
- Transfer mix into the tin, cover with cling film and freeze overnight.
- Crumble the honeycomb over the top just before serving.
- For the cake style version (as per the image above), use the same method as before but put into a 15cm round cake tin. Turn it out and garnish with mixed berries instead of the Crunchie topping if you prefer (see image above).

The Crunchie topping is perfect for a kids' version of this delicious pudding (see main recipe photo)...

GULP WINES RECOMMEND...

The Stump Jump
2010

LEMON & BERRY TART

PREP 20 **MINS**   **COOK** 10 **MINS**

INGREDIENTS (SERVES 4-6)

1 PACK OF READYMADE SHORTCRUST PASTRY
1-2 JARS OF ROSEBUD PRESERVES "LEMON CURD"
100 G BERRIES OF YOUR CHOICE (RIPE FIGS WORK WELL TOO!)
500 ML DOUBLE CREAM (OPTIONAL)
ICING SUGAR TO DUST

METHOD

- Preheat oven to 180°C / Fan 160°C / Gas 4.

- Roll out the readymade shortcrust pastry (or make your own if you prefer) so that it's 4–5mm thick and line an 8 inch pastry mould with it. Allow this to rest for 10–15 minutes.

- Pour your baking beans on top of a baking sheet on top of the pastry for 10 minutes but please follow the instructions on the baking beans packagaing as they can vary.

- Put in your baking beans and check that the pastry bottom is cooked. If not, cook through for a further few minutes until nicely browned on the base. Allow this to cool.

- Fill with the curd and garnish with your fruit of choice. The Rosebud curd is wonderfully lemony and that's why we've said 1-2 jars as this will depend on personal taste. You will see the double cream is optional as a topping before the fruit, should you wish to dull the citrus flavours.

- Dust with icing sugar before serving.

GULP WINES RECOMMEND...
Furleigh Estate Pinot
Chardonnay

ROSEBUD PRESERVES

Rosebud Preserves
MASHAM, YORKSHIRE

Rosebud Preserves headquarters is based in three converted barns at Rosebud Farm. The oldest barn was built in 1830 in the middle of the small village of Healey in North Yorkshire. Situated just south of Wensleydale on the north side of a wide valley with open views across beautiful countryside, it is here the Rosebud team prepares a range of over fifty sweet and savoury preserves.

These are made principally by hand and in small batches using the best available ingredients bought and gathered locally wherever possible. They include wild fruit and flowers picked from the surrounding hedgerows each spring and autumn — crabapples and rowanberries to make fruit jellies and aromatic elderflowers to perfume gooseberry jam. There are damsons from a long established orchard in the Cumbrian Lyth Valley, locally grown herbs, green tomatoes from Lancashire, beetroot and rhubarb from Yorkshire and lots more from the surrounding counties.

The naturally-set fresh herb jellies including Mint, Rosemary, Sage and Thyme — long-time favourites in our domestic market - have achieved outstanding success in the top gourmet and natural food stores across the Atlantic in America. The aim is to capture all the good points of a homemade product by filling the jars with generous quantities of fresh, seasonal ingredients, locally sourced and organic where possible. These are prepared without the addition of additives, preservatives, colourings or gelling agents. The preserves are characterized by bold, fresh flavours and have all the honesty and simplicity of the very best food you can prepare in your own kitchen.

www.rosebudpreserves.co.uk

THE FUDGE KITCHEN

devilishly different

Fudge originates not from Devon or Cornwall, as many people imagine, but legend places its origins at a female college in Virginia, USA. A college lecturer was taking a class in toffee making and the sugar was allowed to recrystallise by accident. The end product was called 'fudge', which is why the term 'fudge' is used to indicate a mistake or error. The USA remains one of the fudge-making centers of the world. For example tiny Mackinac Island off the coast of Michigan has over fourteen fudge shops in just two streets, many dating back to the 19th Century.

Passionate fudge makers since 1983, the Fudge Kitchen is inspired by their heritage and use a recipe dating back to 1830. They still make fudge by hand, on marble slabs and their American-style fudge is made using whipping cream instead of butter, giving a creamy soft texture and distinctive flavour.

All the fudge is freshly made and sold at dedicated shops in Bath, York, Cambridge, Canterbury, Windsor, Edinburgh and Oxford where you can try a free sample and catch a unique fudge making demonstration.

If you can't make it to a shop you can buy fudge online or buy a fudge making kit. Have a go at making your own confectionary at home and experiment with flavours as diverse as coffee to coconut.

www.fudgekitchen.co.uk

STICKY DATE MADELEINES WITH BUTTERSCOTCH SAUCE

PREP 24 **HOURS**   **COOK** 10 **MINS**

INGREDIENTS (MAKES 15)

120G MELTED BUTTER
100G CHOPPED DATES
3 EGGS
120G BROWN SUGAR
175G FLOUR
1 TSP BAKING POWDER

JAR OF THE FUDGE KITCHEN
"BUTTERSCOTCH SAUCE"

METHOD

- Melting the butter and leave to cool. Whisk together the eggs and sugar in a bowl until light and fluffy. Sift in the flour and baking powder gradually. Add melted butter, gently folding the mixture and not stirring too vigorously. Then add your dates and cover bowl with cling film. Refrigerate overnight.

- The next day, preheat the oven to 180°C / Fan 160°C / Gas 4. Grease your madeleine tray (you will need a specific tray for these) generously and sprinkle flour over the top. Pour mixture into the tray — leaving a 1cm gap for rise - bang the tray gently to knock out any air bubbles.

- Bake them for 10 minutes. Remove and leave to cool.

- When you are ready to serve, drizzle generously with the butterscotch sauce and extra sauce for dipping.

GULP WINES RECOMMEND...

The Stump Jump
2010

GRANOLA – KNICKERBOCKER GLORY STYLE

PREP 30 **MINS**   **COOK** 10 **MINS**

INGREDIENTS (SERVES 2-4)

3 STICKS RHUBARB, CHOPPED
2 ORANGES, PEELED & CHOPPED
2 NECTARINES, SKINNED &
CHOPPED
2 PLUMS, SKINNED & CHOPPED
2 PEACHES, SKINNED & CHOPPED

220G CANE GRANULATED SUGAR
220G SCRUMSHUS GRANOLA
220G LOW FAT GREEK YOGHURT
FRUIT & MINT TO DECORATE
– SEE IMAGE FOR INSPIRATION

METHOD

- Put the fruit in a pan over a low heat with the sugar. Stir well until soft and cooked through — about 15 minutes.

- Layer the ingredients into a large glass. Start with the fruit mixture, then the yoghurt, and finally the granola.

- Repeat until you reach the top.

The best effect for the yoghurt is achieved by using a piping bag... if you have one. We think that sliced strawberries look beautiful - place gently around the glass with tongs — top with a sprig of mint.

GULP WINES RECOMMEND...

The Stump Jump

2010

SCRUMSHUS

scrumshus®
— the Premium Granola —

Scrumshus is a premium granola made using the finest natural ingredients. It has been awarded a Great Taste Gold Award 2012 and 2011 by the Guild of Fine Foods , which is a wonderful endorsement of the product.

Scrumshus Granola is made with generous quantities of jumbo oats, coconut, honey, pure maple syrup, almonds, cashew nuts, sunflower seeds, pumpkin seeds, cranberries, raisins and hazelnuts. But, unlike most granolas, it does not contain any fruit juice, added sugar, salt or preservatives. It is quite simply delicious.

Scrumshus Granola is served at some of the most exclusive 5* hotels in the world including Claridges, The Dorchester, The Ritz, The Goring, Gleneagles and many more throughout the UK, as well as many cafes including Carluccio's, Itsu and The Natural Kitchen.

Scrumshus Granola is offered in a PET recyclable, non-glass jar in fine food retailers including Selfridges, Planet Organic and Whole Foods Market and many more throughout the UK, Europe and the Middle East It is also supplied in 1kg bags to hotels and cafes. Scrumshus is KLBD and has Vegetarian Society approval.

www.scrumshus.co.uk

EAT YOUR DRINK

Elderflower, Watermelon,
Lime & Gin Granita
SIPSMITH

Raw Prawns with
Asian Ginseng Dipping Sauce
KAMM AND SONS

BBQ Beer Chicken
BILL'S PRODUCE STORE

Sarsaparilla Vanilla Floats
MAWSON'S

Sloe Lemonade Dessert Slices
BRECKLAND ORCHARD

Espresso Infused Crème Brûlées
HORSHAM COFFEE ROASTERY

Lemon & Thyme Cookies
with Earl Grey Glaze
ROSY LEE TEA

English Mead & Quince Tarte Tartin
LURGASHALL WINERY

Raspberry Vodka Sorbet
NUTMEG FINE FOODS

Crab, Chilli & Sparkling
Wine Linguine
TINWOOD ESTATE

SIPSMITH

SIPSMITH®
independent spirits

Sipsmith by name and nature — after years working in the drinks industry, Sam, Fairfax and Jared struck out on their own to pursue a passion for beautifully handmade spirits. What they make is a celebration of the craft of distillation.

The headquarters in Hammersmith, West London, was once home to the esteemed whisky expert Michael Jackson. Before that it was the micro-brewery for a local pub. Now it is home to Prudence — the first copper still to launch in London for nearly 200 years. Designed by Germany's oldest distillery producers, Christian Carl — a small, family business who have been crafting stills since 1869. She is the only one of her kind in the world.

Inspired by the two hundred years of inherited London distilling history, Sipsmith balance modern technology with traditional recipes and techniques. They make all the spirits by hand in genuinely small numbered batches — just a few hundred bottles a time. They passionately believe this is the only way to craft spirits of this quality. Sipsmith is where old meets new and the two get on really quite spectacularly.

The swan motif on the Sipsmith bottle is a reference to the 'swan's neck' pipe where the spirit vapour turns above the still. It is a representation of the beautiful and elegant Prudence who is at the heart of everything they do. Prudence's bespoke design combining a pot, with a carter head and a column still makes her incredibly versatile, allowing distillation of both Barley Vodka and London Dry Gin from the same still — albeit with a cleaning day in between.

www.sipsmith.com

EAT YOUR DRINK

Add more lime and gin for a more intense granita... this is not a palette cleanser!

ELDERFLOWER, WATERMELON, LIME & GIN GRANITA

PREP 24 **HOURS**   ASSEMBLY 5 **MINS**

INGREDIENTS (SERVES 4-6)

150 ML SIPSMITH GIN
50 ML LIME JUICE
50 ML ELDERFLOWER CORDIAL
500 ML WATERMELON JUICE

METHOD

- Mix all of the ingredients together in a large jug and stir well.

- Pour into a shallow dish — or even a baking tray like we have used here. Freeze it for three hours, and then mix it up with a fork.

- Freeze for another hour and repeat this process two more times, or simply leave overnight. Some granita recipes say to fluff the mixture with a fork and re-freeze repeatedly — or you can just do it once.

- Once it is frozen, scrape it again for a fluffy effect, and serve immediately to get the party started.

GULP WINES RECOMMEND...
Furleigh Estate Classic Cuvée

RAW PRAWNS WITH ASIAN GINSENG DIPPING SAUCE

PREP 24 **HOURS**   ASSEMBLY 10 MINS

INGREDIENTS (SERVES 3-6)

2 TBSP KAMM & SONS
6 TIGER PRAWNS, COOKED
4 TBSP SESAME OIL
- OR REGULAR OIL
2 TBSPS DARK SOY SAUCE
4 SPRING ONIONS

1 CHILLI
1 TBSP BASIL
1 TBSP CORIANDER
SALT & PEPPER
JUICE OF ONE LIME
2 SHALLOTS, FINELY DICED

METHOD

- Combine all of the ingredients and leave the prawns to marinate for 24 hours.
- Serve prawns skewered on sticks and use the remaining marinade as a dip.

serve with shots of Kamm & sons ginseng spirit.

GULP WINES RECOMMEND...

Julian Schaal Chardonnay

2011

EAT YOUR DRINK

KAMM & SONS

Alex Kammerling is a veteran of the drinks industry. For almost 20 years he has worked in bars, restaurants, hotels and nightclubs both in his home town of Bournemouth and in the Orient. Originally intent on being a sculptor, Alex fell in love with the drinks industry and found a flair for creating cocktails. He went on to win numerous cocktail competitions and eventually wrote a book for the BBC. Alex has made drinks for celebrated actors, rock stars, models and royalty and worked with cult brands such as Grey Goose, Schweppes, Campari, Appleton and Martin Miller's gin.

In 2011, after five years research, Alex launched his own brand Kamm & Sons — Ginseng Spirit. This bittersweet botanical spirit can be served as an aperitif over ice or served tall with bitter lemon. It contains a blend of 45 natural botanicals including ginseng, fresh grapefruit peels and manuka honey. Distilled and bottled in London with a distinctive golden hue, the Kamm & Sons taste is complex and distinctive; citrus freshness with light floral, anise and juniper notes giving way to a sweet, rich and herbal palate which ends with a long, honeyed bitterness.

www.kammandsons.com

BILL'S PRODUCE STORE

  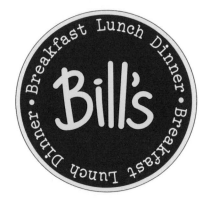

Bill Collison was 22 when his father offered him a shed and told him to make of it what he wished. His father owned a nursery, where Bill had regularly helped out while growing up. So when it came to starting a business Bill did what came naturally and opened a little greengrocers. From humble beginnings it became a bigger greengrocers on the high street. The presentation of the food fascinated him and in direct opposition to pristine supermarket style he arranged his fruit tumbling out of crates as if the farmer had just delivered them from the field.

After several years, Bill's Produce Store and Café was opened in Lewes. By word of mouth it became a success, popular with with locals and a Saturday institution for a food discerning London crowd. The store featured high shelving adorned with different homemade condiments and jams.

The style of the restaurant is cool but laid back. The business has grown and now there are several branches of this easy going restaurant dotted around the South of England. Bill's is the epitome of homegrown rustic produce, loved and cared for, cooked to perfection and delivered to your plate fuss free.

From award-winning breakfasts through to delicious and unusual lunch dishes and the twinkling of candles by night, Bill's is the place to be.

www.bills-website.co.uk

BBQ BEER CHICKEN

PREP 30 **MINS**   **COOK** 30 **MINS**

INGREDIENTS (SERVES 4-6)

4 CHICKEN WINGS, THIGHS OR
DRUMSTICKS
70 G CORN FLOUR
75 ML BILL'S BEER
2 TBSP SOY SAUCE
2 TBSP HONEY

½ TSP CHILLI POWDER
PINCH OF CHILLI FLAKES
PINCH OF SALT
1 TBSP RICE WINE VINEGAR
1 GRATED GARLIC CLOVE

METHOD

- Preheat oven to 220°C / Fan 200°C / Gas 7. Rinse and dry on kitchen paper, then sprinkle the chicken in the corn flour and rub in.

- Mix together the beer, soy, honey, chilli, garlic, flakes, salt and vinegar in a bowl. Drop in the chicken to marinate it in the sauce, making sure it's drenched and cover with cling film.

- Put this in the fridge for quarter of an hour. Then move the chicken from the bowl to an oven proof dish lined with tin foil and cook for 10 minutes.

- Pour the rest of the marinade into a saucepan and reduce for 10 minutes — whilst the chicken is cooking, it should be quite thick in consistency.

- Once this has happened, take the chicken out and brush in the reduced sauce on both sides.

- Return to the oven for another 20 minutes, basting throughout.

GULP WINES RECOMMEND...

Julien Schaal Syrah
2011

SARSAPARILLA VANILLA FLOATS

PREP 2 **MINS**   **ASSEMBLY** 2 **MINS**

INGREDIENTS (MAKES I)

½ BOTTLE MAWSON'S "SPARKLING SARSAPARILLA"
I SCOOP VANILLA ICE CREAM

METHOD

- Once you have picked a pretty glass, we used an old-style sundae glass, pour in the sparkling sasparelli and then add a large scoop of vanilla ice cream (or you could use plain frozen yoghurt)... and voilà!

If you haven't tried sarsaparilla, then do so! It's different (and better than) traditional root beer - and much more interesting than Coca-Cola!

GULP WINES RECOMMEND...
Furleigh Estate Classic Cuvée

MAWSON'S

The story of Mawson's Sarsaparilla began in 1933, when milkman Joe Mawson bought a herbalist's shop in Oldham. Joe's backroom, with its piano and card tables ,was soon a popular meeting place for local people. In his cellar Joe brewed forty gallons a day of non-alcoholic beer from a mixture of more than twenty herbs. The concoction was sold for 4d a pint.

When Joe's first opened there were twenty temperance bars in Oldham, a firmly established part of the social scene. For members of the free churches it provided an alternative drinking parlour with family appeal. An increase in licensed bars meant its popularity dwindled and by 1963 last orders was called for the final time.

Now, three generations later, Mawson's sell their Sarsaparilla in a cordial form for you to enjoy at home. Produced by the same family and to the original recipe, Mawson's Sarsaparilla Cordial is made from natural ingredients, including ginger, liquorice and sarsaparilla. Dilute to taste with either still or sparkling spring water and enjoy it hot in the winter months. Mawson's refreshingly original Sarsaparilla non-alcoholic tipple of Sass 'n Soda is back.

www.teastudio.co.uk

BRECKLAND ORCHARD

Breckland Orchard

When Claire Martinsen made the life-changing decision to go into business for herself, she looked to her grandmother for inspiration. "When I started Breckland Orchard I wanted to recreate the refreshing tastes of my childhood," she says. "Granny's lemonade was legendary, bursting with flavour."

The company's signature Lemonade is a classic Posh Pop — clean and crisp tasting and one sip will have your whole mouth bursting with flavour. Made with real fruit, no artificial colours, flavours or sweeteners, it led the way for 7 more countryside-inspired flavours including gold star winner at the Great Tastes Award, Strawberry and Rhubarb. Summer in a bottle all year round!

Like every small business owner, Claire performs a myriad of roles at Breckland Orchard. "I make absolutely no apologies for that," she says. "I adore thinking up new flavour combinations, which come from my deep rooted love of cooking and experimenting with different tastes. I love baking, making jams and chutneys, messing around in the kitchen. I adore things like that... I carry that passion into all the new flavours and products." Latest to hit the shelves is a range of super concentrated cordials.

www.brecklandorchard.co.uk

SLOE LEMONADE DESSERT SLICES

PREP 35 **MINS**   **COOK** 45 **MINS**

INGREDIENTS (MAKES 15)

50 G SUGAR
½ LEMON ZEST
1 TSP SALT
115 G BUTTER
125 G FLOUR

FOR THE TOPPING

140 G RASPBERRIES
2 EGGS
150 G SUGAR
100 ML BRECKLAND ORCHARD
"SLOE LEMONADE"
40 G ICING SUGAR, FOR DUSTING

METHOD

- Preheat oven to 180°C / Fan 160°C / Gas 4. Grease an oven tin and cover with baking parchment.

- Whisk together the sugar, lemon zest, salt and butter until it makes a dough. Add the flour until crumbly. Press this mixture down into the pan, prick with a fork, and push up the sides of the tray by 1cm. Bake this for 15 minutes. Then leave to cool.

- Liquidise the raspberries and sieve to remove any pips. In another bowl mix the eggs, sugar, and lemonade until smooth. Add 3 tbsp. of the raspberry juice.

- Pour this onto the pre-cooked crust, and bake for 30 minutes (or until set).

- Leave to cool before slicing into pieces. You can do this in the fridge. Sprinkle with icing sugar to serve. Goes well with a glass of cool Sloe Lemonade.

GULP WINES RECOMMEND...
Prosecco Dolci Colline

ESPRESSO INFUSED CRÈME BRÛLÉES

PREP *5* **HOURS**   **COOK** *20* **MINS**

INGREDIENTS (MAKES 4-6)

4 EGG YOLKS
75 G HORSHAM "COFFEE BEANS", GROUND AT HOME
75 G CASTER SUGAR
1 TSP VANILLA EXTRACT
6 TSP DEMERARA SUGAR FOR GLAZING

METHOD

- Preheat oven to 150°C / Fan 130°C / Gas 2.

- Mix 250ml of the cream and sugar in a saucepan over a medium heat. Add the ground coffee and bring to the boil whilst stirring gently.

- Take this off the heat and leave to steep for 5 minutes for the coffee to infuse.

- Place a tea towel in the bottom of a roasting tin, and put your ramekins (or we used espresso cups) on top.

- Boil the kettle. Once steeped, pour in the rest of the cream. Whisk your egg yolks and vanilla in a separate bowl. Gradually add the cream until it is all thoroughly mixed together and then pass through a very fine sieve.

- Make sure there are no hard bits floating around, and then evenly distribute the cream into your dishes. Put the tin in the oven, and then pour boiling water from your kettle into the tin until covering your dishes about 2/3 of the way. Bake these for 25 minutes, or until the brûlées have just set.

- Take out of the oven, leave to cool. Once cool, cover with cling film and refrigerate for at least 4 hours.

- When ready, sprinkle with Demerara sugar. Caramelise with a blowtorch. Refrigerate for a further 30 minutes before serving.

GULP WINES RECOMMEND...

The Stump Jump

2010

EAT YOUR DRINK

HORSHAM COFFEE ROASTER

HORSHAM
COFFEE
ROASTER

Bradley Steenkamp spent his formative teenage years drinking gallons of addictive Tim Hortons coffee in Canada (despite being originally from South Africa — it's a long story). As his palette matured he started to crave something that tasted a bit more like real coffee. Bradley moved to the UK in 2001 and found the coffee experience a tad disappointing. Over the next 10 years he watched with interest as specialist coffee shops began gaining popularity in nearby Brighton and London. In 2011, during a work secondment to Canada, Bradley and his wife Amelia noticed the business potential behind their love of ethically sourced and freshly roasted coffee.

During Bradley's 10-year absence Canada had developed a coffee culture and it was at the Green Beanery in Toronto they bought their first small batch of green beans. At home, with the constant fear of setting off the fire alarm, they used a popcorn popper to roast these first batches to give as Christmas presents to friends. The arrival of a baby in 2011 meant a change of priorities for Amelia so she started designing the logo and all creative aspects of the business. As soon as they returned to England, Bradley concentrated on researching everything he could find online about coffee roasting, cupping, grinding and generally becoming a coffee bore.

After setting up the Toper Roaster in the ex-garage and buying all the suitable espresso machines, grinders, etc. Horsham Coffee Roaster was officially launched in June 2012 at Horsham's new Thursday market. Although family and friends were originally the most loyal customers this has been replaced by like-minded locals who want good quality, fresh coffee that doesn't come from a chain. Now Horsham Coffee Roaster supplies numerous small local shops, farm shops and cafes. A visit to the London Coffee Festival proved to them their coffee truly matches up in quality and flavour to London based roasters that have been around much longer. From the high level of exposure they have gained wholesale supply from further afield. However, they are still passionate about local supply and want to find other businesses who share their love of quality coffee as much as they do.

www.horshamcoffeeroaster.com

ROSY LEE TEA

Rosy Lee Tea London wanted to make and sell a decent British cup of tea that not only tasted great but looked great on the shelf too. They had a passion for two things — tea and London. It made sense to name the brand using London's famous secret language — Cockney Rhyming Slang.

Fancy a cup of Rosy Lee? – Cockney rhyming slang for the classic and much loved British cup of tea. Celebrating London in every cup, all Rosy Lee Tea London teas are full bodied and great tasting — perfect for anytime of the day.

The man in the button covered suit, or 'Pearly', you can see on the packaging is part of a tradition started in the 19th Century in the East End of London. Now a unique part of London culture Rosy Lee Tea London are happy to donate a percentage of their sales to charity through the Pearly Society. Rosy Lee Tea London's range of teas is sold in beautiful tins and is a cupboard and cafe favourite.

Rosy Lee the Londoners' Tea — warming the cockles of ya heart!

www.rosyleetealondon.com

LEMON & THYME COOKIES WITH EARL GREY GLAZE

PREP 1 **HR** 30 **MINS**   **COOK** 20 **MINS**

INGREDIENTS (MAKES 25)

220 G BUTTER
150 G SUGAR
470 G FLOUR
A FEW SPRIGS OF DRIED THYME
½ TSP SALT
220 G ICING SUGAR

3 TBSP ROSY LEE TEA'S
"PEARLY GREY" – BREWED TO
TWICE ITS NORMAL STRENGTH

METHOD

- Mix together the butter and sugar. Add the lemon zest.

- In a separate bowl, mix the flour, thyme and salt. Combine this with the butter and sugar.

- Roll the dough into a cookie sized log. Then roll in cling film and refrigerate for about an hour.

- Preheat the oven to 150°C / Fan 130°C / Gas 2. Slice cookie sized circles off the end of the log and place on an oven proof tin covered with baking parchment. Make sure that none of the cookies are touching. Put these in the oven for 20 minutes, or until turning golden.

- Take out and leave to cool.

- Mix the icing sugar and earl grey tea to make a glaze. Spoon this over the cookies once they are cooled. Garnish with thyme leaves, and enjoy with a cup of Pearly Grey!

GULP WINES RECOMMEND...

Auramis Vermentino
2011

ENGLISH MEAD & QUINCE TARTE TARTIN

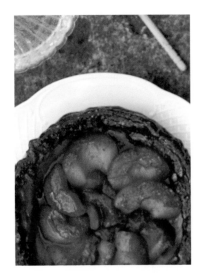

PREP 45 **MINS**   **COOK** 45 **MINS**

INGREDIENTS (SERVES 4-6)

3 QUINCES, PEELED & QUARTERED
½ LEMON
1 CINNAMON STICK
400 ML LURGASHALL MEAD
100G SUGAR

1 PACKET OF ALL BUTTER PUFF PASTRY
2 TSP BROWN SUGAR
4 TBSP QUINCE PASTE (FIND THIS IN THE CHEESE SECTION OF THE SUPERMARKET!)

METHOD

- Put the water, mead, sugar, lemon juice, cinnamon stick, fruit (quince or other) and half the quince paste into a saucepan over a low heat. Put a circular piece of greaseproof paper over the top (ensuring that there is a hole in the middle for steam) and cook for 30 minutes, checking and shaking if necessary.

- Preheat oven to 190°C / Fan 170°C / Gas 5. Put 250ml of the poaching liquid into an oven proof frying pan with the remaining quince paste and simmer. Then position your fruit in a circular motion — much like we have. Try to make sure there aren't too many gaps.

- Flour your kitchen top, and then roll out your pastry into a circular shape, just bigger than the pan. Lay this over the saucepan and tuck it in at the sides.

- Bake this for 45 minutes, until crisp and golden. Then leave to cool for 10 minutes before turning over using a plate.

- Serve immediately, although we think it tastes best after a day in the fridge.

GULP WINES RECOMMEND...

Chamonix Blanc

2011

We found a great quince paste with some damson in - and this was great!

LURGASHALL WINERY

Lurgashall Winery nestles in a 38-acre estate beneath Blackdown Hills, the highest point in West Sussex. It is housed in award-winning 17th and 19th century farm buildings, whose rustic style complements the country nature of the products.

Now a family run business, director and one of three owners of Lurgashall Winery, Sarah Thompson is excited to be at the helm. "As a family we knew the previous owner and my father Steve even helped with the rebuild of the original barn in which the winery is housed. As soon as we knew the business had become available we decided to take on the challenge. We did not want to see a good, well known English product come to an end and a stunning property be converted into flats. This is such a unique opportunity, we knew that we would not regret taking it on."

Ian Morris, Head Wine Maker, has been with the winery for over 30 years. His duties are to ensure that the diverse range remains of the highest quality and standard whilst safeguarding the traditional and lost art of wine making.

With this expertise, Lurgashall is proud to offer traditional English liqueurs, Meads and Country Wines. Made only from the finest natural ingredients, none of which are touched by any essences, flavourings or artificial ingredients. Suitable for vegetarians and vegans (with the exception of Mead).

Lurgashall seasonally produces approximately 20 varieties, the most popular being Silver Birch Wine, Elderflower Wine, Elderberry Port and Meads. "We currently have 38 acres of Silver Birch Trees on our land which we tap for sap when it is rising between February and March. We use the land for other ingredients and source everything else locally," says Sarah. "We would love to have our own hives but can use in excess 8 tons of honey per year so we source our honey for the Mead from Payne's Honey Farm in Hassocks, Sussex."

www.lurgashall.co.uk

NUTMEG FINE FOODS

Nutmeg's founder, Ann Goodwin, has always been passionate about food. Spending holidays with her grandparents in Antwerp, Belgium, she fondly remembers being taken to the local markets to choose and taste all they had to offer and those evocative smells still remain a treasured memory. The freshness and quality of local produce being the keystones to the Belgian way of life and their cooking.

Many years later, Ann was inspired to share her love of cooking and good food so she set up Nutmeg Fine Foods. Based in Petersfield, Ann and her team are committed to providing the very best handmade food, using only fresh, quality ingredients that, wherever possible, are locally sourced and seasonal. Everything from frozen meals, puddings and quiches to ready prepared picnics, chutneys and dressings are handmade.

Nutmeg attend a number of fairs throughout the year to offer tastings of their produce and to sell pâtés, chutneys, dressings, tarts and quiches as well as Nutmeg's best selling Raspberry Vodka and Sloe Gin. Everything is available to buy either individually or as part of a superb hamper or gift box and make wonderful presents.

Nutmeg Fine Foods have recently expanded their range of frozen food to include a choice of delicious puddings which are now available to buy at selected local retail outlets, as well as via the website.

www.nutmegfinefoods.co.uk

RASBERRY VODKA SORBET

PREP 2 HRS 20 **MINS**   **ASSEMBLY** 5 **MINS**

INGREDIENTS (SERVES 6-8)

300 G RASPBERRIES
100 ML WATER
100 ML NUTMEG FINE FOODS "RASPBERRY VODKA"
100 G SUGAR
1 LIME SQUEEZED

METHOD

- Put the water, sugar and vodka in a saucepan over a low heat to dissolve the sugar. Allow to cool.

- Liquidise the raspberries and lime, and then pass though a sieve to get rid of pips. Combine the syrup and the fruit puree.

- You can put this in an ice cream machine if you have one. If you don't, then place the mix in a shallow tray in the freezer, and stir by hand every 30 minutes for the first 2 hours.

- Serve whenever you like.

GULP WINES RECOMMEND...

Chamonix Blanc
2011

CRAB, CHILLI & SPARKLING WINE LINGUINE

PREP 20 **MINS**   **COOK** 20 **MINS**

INGREDIENTS (SERVES 2)

250 G LINGUINE

1 TBSP OLIVE OIL

1 CHOPPED LEEK

1 CHILLI, CHOPPED & DE-SEEDED

2 SLICED GARLIC CLOVES

4 CHOPPED MEDIUM TOMATOES

1 TSP CHOPPED GINGER

1 POT OF CRAB MEAT

TINWOOD WINE, BIG SPLASH

½ LIME JUICE

HANDFUL OF FRESH

CHOPPED CORIANDER

METHOD

- Cook the linguine to instructions on the packet.

- Heat the oil in a large pan. Add the chilli, leek, garlic and ginger and fry for 5 minutes. Add the tomatoes, crab and a generous splash of the sparkling wine. Simmer and stir the sauce, cooking through for 10 minutes. If it looks too dry, then add another dash of wine.

- Once the pasta is done and drained, add the sauce and mix well. Serve into bowls and garnish with coriander and a squeeze of the lime juice. Absolutely serve this with the rest of the wine.

GULP WINES RECOMMEND...

Tinwood Estate Sparkling Wine

THE TINWOOD ESTATE

The Tinwood Estate is situated in West Sussex at the foot of the South Downs National Park. The Downs protect the vineyard from the North and East while importantly the sea, 5 miles away, keeps much of the frost away early in the season. The farm is in the rain shadow of the Isle of Wight and has a unique microclimate and is repeatedly named as the sunniest place in Great Britain — over 1,900 hours of sunshine in 2011.

The Farm has 3 vineyards. The oldest was planted in 2008 and is called House vineyard due to its proximity to the farm house. House vineyard can be seen directly in front of the tasting room and compromises of 48% Chardonnay, 32% Pinot Noir and 20% Pinot Meunier. The next vineyard, Ounces Barn, compromises 55% Chardonnay, 26% Pinot Noir and 19% Pinot Meunier. The name comes from old maps which show many years ago there was a barn here called Ounces. Finally, Oma's block which is entirely pinot noir. This vineyard can be seen when entering Tinwood Lane. Currently we have three different wines available: Tinwood Estate Brut 2010, Tinwood Estate Rose 2010 and Tinwood Estate Blanc de Blanc 2010.

Tinwood have built a brand new, modern tasting room overlooking the vines, so why not pop by for a glass of wine with a beautiful view.

www.tinwoodestate.com

POCKET PICNICS
AND SUBTLE FEASTING

Vanilla Yogurt Covered
Cranberries & Goji Berries
TIMS DAIRY

Rose Water Scones
WEETONS

Kiwi, Lemon, Elderflower
& Earl Grey Marmalade Muffins
JAMSMITH

Frozen Banana
& Cacao Nibbles
BOOJA-BOOJA

Popcorn Lollies
PETER POPPLE'S POPCORN

TIMS DAIRY

Established in London in 1949 by Euripides Nicolaou and subsequent partner Michael Timotheou, uncle and father of the present owners, Tims Dairy was always always has been a family business. It began by making homemade, natural yogurts and desserts which they supplied to local, ethnic coffee bars, continental delicatessens and restaurants. The family business has grown from there.

Now run by the four Timotheou brothers, Tims Dairy value their Greek heritage and pride themselves on creating wholesome, fresh live yogurts.

Over the years many customers made contact having eaten their yogurts in hotels, schools and hospitals. The brothers knew they had to develop a retail range. From 2009 their fabulous product was available in shops and included delicious, authentic Greek style, wholemilk and low fat natural and fruit yogurts and a 4-pack for children called Tiny Tims. All of Tims Dairy yogurts are made with natural ingredients and use only fresh British milk and cream.

Restaurateur Yotam Ottolenghi believes, "Cooking in yogurt produces fantastic results that can be exceptionally exciting." Another fan is Athens born and celebrated London chef Theodore Kyriakou who now considers Tims Dairy Greek style yogurts to be the best this side of the Aegean.

Having moved away from central and then north London, the dairy has been located in the heart of the beautiful Chiltern Hills in Chalfont St. Peter, Buckinghamshire, since 1996.

www.timsdairy.co.uk

VANILLA YOGURT CRANBERRIES & GOJI BERRIES

PREP 6 **HOURS**   ASSEMBLY 5 MINS

INGREDIENTS (SERVES 4)

110 G DRIED CRANBERRIES

110 G DRIED GOJI BERRIES

1 TBSP WATER

1 TSP VANILLA EXTRACT

60 ML TIMS DAIRY "NATURAL" OR
"VANILLA GREEK" YOGURT

1 TBSP HONEY

200 G ICING SUGAR

METHOD

- Combine the yogurt, honey, salt and vanilla essence. Heat briefly (either in microwave stirring frequently or on the hob) to make the yogurt liquidy but do not boil or curdle the mixture.

- Put the yogurt back into a bowl; add the sugar and mix. Coat the cranberries and goji berries with a light dusting of icing sugar, and then pour half of the yogurt on top, and stir all of the fruit in.

- Separate the berries on some baking parchment and leave to set for half an hour. Then repeat the process again, so that they get a good thick coating. Once coated for the second time, put them back on a clean piece of baking parchment, being careful to separate them.

- There are two options with this dish — have them frozen or dry them out to eat later. They usually take 6 hours to dry. Store at room temperature.

GULP WINES RECOMMEND...

Furleigh Estate Classic Cuvée

If you decide to go for a frozen snack, they should not take more than 2 hours to freeze but then eat them immediately!

ROSE WATER SCONES

PREP 15 **MINS**   **COOK** 10 **MINS**

INGREDIENTS (MAKES 6)

100 ML WEETONS "ROSE WATER"   1 TSP BICARBONATE OF SODA
165 G FLOUR   1 TSP CREAM OF TARTAR
50 ML MILK
3 TBSP HONEY
20 G BUTTER
PINCH SALT

METHOD

- Preheat the oven to 220°C / Fan 200°C / Gas 7.

- Sift the flour, bicarbonate of soda and cream of tartar in a bowl. Rub in the butter. Add the milk, rose water and honey so that it turns into a soggy dough-like mixture.

- Flour your kitchen surface. Knead the dough until the flour stops it from being sticky. Roll and cut out your scones – should be able to do 6 fairly big ones.

- Bake these for 10 minutes, until golden brown.

- To make the rose glaze, put the remaining 50ml rose water in a pan with sugar and gently heat. Stir until it thickens. Don't let it burn. Leave to cool, then use a culinary brush to paint on your glaze on top of your scones.

- Serve with a pot of tea.

GULP WINES RECOMMEND...
Prosecco Dolci Colline

WEETONS

Conceived as a farm shop in 2005, Weetons of Harrogate has established itself in the hearts of food lovers in the locality and further afield. They made their name through the provision of superb local products, especially premium meats; and by establishing long term relationships with farmers, growers and suppliers. Under new ownership, Weetons really has come of age as a Premium Food Hall.

It is a true food destination where customers can shop, enjoy a coffee or dine in the new Restaurant, all in the presence of food expertise. As the purveyors of fine food & drink the ethos is an unerring passion for premium produce, supplied by a select few, small-scale, high-quality independent producers. To satisfy the sophisticated palates of discerning customers they also search far and wide for those extra-special products that make Weetons so unique. Whether from near or far the provenance of everything on offer is second to none. Weetons take pride in knowing, not only where all their stock has come from, but also who produced it; and in providing an exceptional customer experience every day.

With a new online offering, customers can really enjoy the Weetons experience in store or from the comfort of their own home.

www.weetons.com

JAMSMITH

JAMSMITH

After having a child Vicky Smith wanted a job to fit in around family life. So when she was offered a remote, old house in Wensleydale for a peppercorn rent in 2006, she left London. It was while out exploring and taking photographs of the local countryside she noticed the abundance of wild fruit in the hedgerows behind her house. She taught herself to make preserves taking inspiration from the traditional skills of the farming community around her.

Having mastered the basics she sold her jams at local fairs and markets. Then she began experimenting with unusual flavour combinations such as Summer Pudding with Elderflower jam and Foraged Wild Sloe, Crabapple and Bramble jelly. She honed her technique and found a niche for the special, high fruit content, soft-set jams she was making.

Soon friends were asking to be sent products regularly, either for themselves or as gifts to others. The JAMSMITH monthly subscription idea was born. Once a month Vicky makes two unique jams, jellies or marmalades using only top quality, fresh, seasonal fruit adding herbs or spices for further interest and depth. Some ingredients she picks from within walking distance of her house, other fruits are sourced from local gardeners and a weekly farmers' market.

At JAMSMITH each jar is personalised by hand with the jam club member's name on the label, packaged up and posted with tasting notes and monthly recipe suggestions to customers all over the UK.

JAMSMITH is a "seasonal preserves by subscription" company based in the Yorkshire Dales run by Vicky Smith.

www.jamsmith.co.uk

KIWI, LEMON, ELDERFLOWER & EARL GREY MARMALADE MUFFINS Ⓥ

PREP 20 **MINS**   **COOK** 20 **MINS**

INGREDIENTS (MAKES 10 - 12)

100 G JAMSMITH "KIWI, LEMON, ELDERFLOWER & EARL GREY MARMALADE"
175 G SELF RAISING FLOUR
½ TSP BAKING POWDER
PINCH OF SALT

4 TBSP CASTER SUGAR
2 TBSP ORANGE JUICE
1 BEATEN EGG
3 TBSP BUTTER
150 ML MILK

METHOD

- Preheat the oven to 220°C / Fan 200°C / Gas 7.

- Sift the flour, powder, sugar and salt into a bowl. Separately, mix the marmalade together with the orange juice. Make a dip in the middle of the flour and add the egg, oil, marmalade and the milk, and then quickly fold together with the butter.

- Once well combined, spoon the mixture into the cases and bake for 20 minutes, or until light and fluffy to touch.

Paddington would love these and would definitely have been a member of the Jamsmith club!

GULP WINES RECOMMEND...
The Stump Jump

FROZEN BANANA & CACAO NIBBLES

PREP 1 HR 15 MINS   **ASSEMBLY** 5 MINS

INGREDIENTS (MAKES 6)

1 PACKET OF BOOJA-BOOJA "CACAO NIBS"
1 BANANA
3 TBSP DAIRY FREE NATURAL YOGHURT
SPRINKLING OF TOASTED HAZELNUTS

METHOD

- Chop your banana into thick slices. Dip in the dairy free yoghurt and coat. Place them on a piece of foil and put in the freezer for an hour.
- Sprinkle with raw cacao nibs and toasted hazelnuts.
- Serve frozen and watch out because they melt quickly!

GULP WINES RECOMMEND...

The Stump Jump

POCKET PICNICS AND SUBTLE FEASTING

197

Note to self:
• Never eat more
than cacao drink
mask contains and
read more Vanity Fair!

BOOJA-BOOJA

Booja-Booja is rather special for several reasons. It is a luxurious, British chocolate company based in Norfolk and one of the few artisan chocolatiers who make their scrumptious truffles by hand. Best known for their melt in the mouth chocolate truffles, Booja-Booja also offers 5 delicious flavours of frozen dessert. This award-winning alternative to dairy ice cream is made with creamy cashew nuts.

The Ecuadorian Criollo Cacao Beans and Cacao Nibs are widely considered to be the finest of their kind and are a perfect addition to smoothies, granola, porridge or as a snack in their own right. A true superfood they have a full, aromatic, rich flavour and are packed with natural mood boosters to uplift body and mind.

Booja-Booja products not only taste exquisite but are also full of good things; the entire range is organic and free from dairy, gluten, soya and, wherever possible, Booja-Booja use only raw ingredients. Their Raw Ecuadorian Dark Truffles and Raw Ecuadorian Raspberry Truffles are the result of a collaboration with Pacari chocolate in Ecuador, a joint product development that was five years in the making. It has resulted in the first ever chocolate to be produced for export by cacao farmers in the country.

Thirteen years and fifty eight awards after the launch of their first truffle, the team at Booja-Booja still consists of passionate and enthusiastic chocolate lovers who love to create utterly delicious, practically guilt-free recipes from the heart and soul.

www.boojabooja.com

PETER POPPLE'S POPCORN

Peter Popple's Popcorn is a fun and tasty snack which proves healthy does not need to be boring. Great for all the family it comes in four flavours: Salt & Vinegar, Golden Syrup, Cheddar Cheese and Tangy Tomato.

Different and healthier from other popcorn and crisps it is air popped, which means it is not cooked in lots of greasy oils. It is lower in salt and fat (8% compared to 19-25% in others) and has only 80 calories per bag.

"There was a gap in the market for a balanced, fun, healthy and tasty snack, so we conducted trials with flavours and ingredients to create something that was a real alternative to crisps and regular salty snacks" says Louise George, the founder of Peter Popple's Popcorn. "We worked hard to create something that kids, mums and dads would love — we say it's popalicious!"

The brand is based on Peter Popple, a young scientist who loves everything that goes pop and the science behind it, but out of all of his experiments Peter's passion is making the perfect popcorn. A Peter Popple's Popcorn cookbook has been published with ideas for popcorn in the park, parties, movie nights as well as the lunch box.

It is low fat and light in texture so it doesn't fill kids up in place of a regular meal but does leave you feeling fuller for longer than most snacks. It even has a dose of B vitamins to boost your energy levels. Peter Popple's Popcorn is on sale in farm shops, local delicatessens and online.

www.peterpopples.com

POPCORN LOLLIES

(V)

PREP 25 **MINS**   **ASSEMBLY** 5 **MINS**

INGREDIENTS (MAKES 6)

2 PACKETS OF PETER POPPLE'S "GOLDEN SYRUP" POPCORN
110 G HARD CARAMEL SWEETS, LIKE "WERTHER'S ORIGINALS"
2 TBSP BUTTER
300 G CHOCOLATE CHIPS
HUNDREDS & THOUSANDS, FOR DIPPING
1 PACK OF LOLLY STICKS

METHOD

- Put the caramel sweets and butter in a saucepan and cook over a low heat until smooth.
- Pour this over the popcorn in a separate bowl, and make sure it is well coated. Leave this to stand for a few minutes.
- Melt your chocolate chips in the microwave, or over the hob. Shape the popcorn into balls – this should make 6.
- Stick in your lolly stick and dip each one in the melted chocolate.
- Sprinkle with hundreds and thousands (you could have some help from the kids here), and then leave to set on baking parchment.

GULP WINES RECOMMEND...

Champagne Louis Brochet
(Adults Only!)

What a recipe to end with...
Boom! Chicka! Pop!

THANK YOU, THANK YOU, THANK YOU!

My written thank you's are on the following pages, but here are same faces to put to some of the names - just some of the totally delicious people in my life that I have had the pleasure to work with on this book...

Paul

Tory

my kitchen scales

Notte

Mark

Lucinda & Niki

Harriet

...try as I might, some of the people on my
thank you list are camera-shy!

THANK, THANK YOU, THANK YOU!

There are so many wonderful people to thank...

This book is the epitome of team work. The book would not have happened unless **The Rare Brand Market** had unearthed the rare brands involved. So my first thank you should go to them. You are all brilliant in your own right and I wish you all the success in the world with your businesses. Some of you have already graduated from doing events like ours to launch your business. Some of you have even recently made it on the shelves of a top London Food halls like **Fortnum and Mason** and **Selfridges** or even some of you into **Waitrose**. Some of you supply the best restaurants and hotels in the world and some of you are preferred by the best chefs in the world. With this in mind I am totally filled with pride that you have agreed to be in this book. By being in this book, I really feel you are part of the best **UK** directory for artisan food producers available today.

Harriet (Rare Brand Scout), you have been my professional right with this book. Thank you for all your patience and unbelievable support.

Tory and Paul, what a double act you are. Rhian — www.illuminatedcanvas.co.uk (another rare brand family member), thanks for introducing Tory and Paul to me. I could not have wished to work with two more talented and fabulous professionals. You both are such experts in your fields, Paul I still can't get over you never once made a mistake during the shoot week, when we cooked and shot 55 dishes in 6 days! You are both geniuses.

Molly, who I have incidently renamed "Marvelous Molly" is quite simply once of the best if not the best graphic designers I have ever worked with, and I have worked with many over the years. Molly and I worked so well together. I have since asked her to be the "resident" graphic design for **The Rare Brand Market**, so that she helps us with all our projects. Molly's ability to work with the "client" and crunch through brief's balancing "client" creative views is uncommon. In the creative industry "creatives" are too often overly opinionated about their own visual direction and style. Molly, I look forward to working with you more and more.

Benson, thank you for your professionalism but especially for helping us to work to such tight timescales.

Becs, thanks for helping us. Your wisdom and decisive strength has been formidable.

Debbie, owner of **Sorbet Living** — www.sorbetliving.com — and **Danny**, owner of **Bloomingville** — www.bloomingvillestore.co.uk — (both rare brand family members) thank you so much for loaning us lots of stunning products as props for our photo shoot. I was very fussy about who I wanted to use, and your ranges were absolutely perfect!

Mariella and Willie, owners of **Southend Barns** — www.southendfarms.co.uk — thank you so much for creating such a perfect and stunning venue for our **Rare Brand Markets**. Also, thank you for letting us do our "cookbook team photo" at the barns — the shot makes a great inside cover!

Noel, Roger and Mark thank you for being so patient... you know why!

Dave and Lisa, my gorgeous sister and brother-in-law. Thank you for fitting in the time to cross-check the edits. Those extra pairs of eyes looking at the details. I am so grateful to you for this. You are both such "givers" and I love you so much.

Lucinda and Niki, my two totally beautiful in every way girlfriends. You have both been an amazing sounding board, you have cooked recipes to test them for me and you have loaned me so many props from your precious personal china and glass collections!!! We have such fun together and you are both such amazing friends — thank you for the help that you have given me with this book and your friendship — I thank you from the bottom of my heart.

My lovely mum, thank you for inspiring me so young to cook and enjoy food. With this in mind and many many other things, where would I be without you...

My wonderful girls, you are the best little chefs I know. Some of my happiest moments with you are cooking in the kitchen together. Let's do more and more. Let's open that cake shop together! Keep looking for empty shops for us in Chichester! Keep pulling out recipes for us to try. **Lorenza,** make sure you do fulfil your dream over being on Junior Master Chef. **Estelle,** your blackberry and banana smoothie invention is the best. **Greta,** keep making the mess you make in the kitchen, never let anyone say to you a goof chef is not a messy chef. I love you three so much.

Mark, you are quite simply my anchor. Your love and support is endless. As you know, I really do thank my lucky stars I found you...

Must also thank the most patient dogs in the world - our dog, Notte, and Paul & Tory's dog, Sullivan - who were so good when the photo shoot took place and all of the lovely aromas were wafting above their noses!

GULP WINES

GULPWINES

EMMA, CLARE & JAMES, GULP WINES

Wine — you know which colour and how much you have to spend, but really what you'd love is for someone to help you choose. Which bottle is the most delicious, suits your budget and complements your meal? That is exactly what **Gulp Wines** does.

Between Emma and Clare, owners of **Gulp** they have five children, six chickens, three dogs, a pony, two cats and a pair of Dorset gardens — badly in need of weeding. They have little children, big children, school-runs, meals to cook, mouths to feed, houses to keep, and gardens to feel guilty about. Like most busy people they still love to host a dinner party or invite a bunch of girlfriends round for a gossip and a glass of something tasty to drink.

The sommelier behind the **Gulp** brand is James Handford. One of only 300 Masters of Wine in the world, with over 25 years of wine buying experience, he has handpicked a selection of just thirty superb wines. From this well-focused snapshot of the best wines on the market **Gulp** was created.

Gulp Wines provide a small, simple, online, jargon-free, unpompous window into the world of excellent affordable wine. The wine chooser feature helps you choose by colour, occasion, budget or accompanying dish.

www.gulpwines.com

WINE LIST

REDS

ROBERT MAS VIC ROUGE 2011, PAYS D'OC SOUTHERN FRANCE £6.59
Blend Grenache, Cinsault, Syrah, Merlot, Cabernet sauvignon 12.5%

CONVIVIALE MONTEPULCIANO 2011, ITALY £6.99
Sangiovese 13.5%

PARVA RES NERO D'AVOLA 2011, SICILY £7.25
Nero d'Avola 13%

ROC D'OPALE 2011, PAYS D'OC, SOUTHERN FRANCE £7.40
Grenache Noir, Merlot. 12.5%

INDOMITA COSTA VERA MERLOT 2011, CHILE £7.49
Merlot 13%. Chile

LA LINDA MALBEC 2011, ARGENTINA £8.99
Malbec 14%

SANTA DUC 2010, GIGONDAS, FRANCE £9.35
Grenache, Syrah, Merlot, Cabernet Sauvignon 14%

BODEGAS MEDIEVO SELECCION ESPECIAL 2010, RIOJA, SPAIN £9.75
Tempranillo 13%

CHATEAU LA TOUR SAINT PAUL 2010, BORDEAUX, FRANCE £9.75
Merlot, Cabernet Sauvignon, Cabernet Franc 13%

QUINCHO CABERNET SAUVIGNON 2010, CHILE £9.99
Cabernet Sauvignon 13.5%

DOMAINE ST JACQUES D'ALBA 2010, LANGUEDOC, FRANCE £9.75
Syrah, Grenache, Mourvedre 14%

PUY DE DOME 2010, FRANCE £9.99
Pinot Noir 13.5%

PITCHFORK SHIRAZ 2009, WESTERN AUSTRALIA £11.95
Shiraz 14%

BROUILLY ST ENNEMOND 2010, BEAUJOLAIS, FRANCE £12.75
Gamay 13%

JULIAN SCHAAL SYRAH 2010, ELGIN, SOUTH AFRICA £12.75
Syrah 14%

VIRGINIE THUNEVIN 2009, BORDEAUX, FRANCE £13.60
Merlot, Cabernet Sauvignon, Cabernet Franc 14%

ROSÉ

LA BELLE PIERRE ROSE 2011, SOUTHERN FRANCE £9.49
Grenache 12.5%
Gold Medal in Paris 2012.

SWEET

THE STUMP JUMP, AUSTRALIA £9.75
Chardonnay, Riesling, Semillon, Pinot Gris and Botrytis 10.5%

WINE LIST

SPARKLING

PROSECCO DOLCI COLLINE BRUT, ITALY £8.45
Prosecco 11.5%

LOUIS BROCHET CHAMPAGNE, FRANCE £24.25
Pinot Noir, Pinot Meunier, Chardonnay 12%

FURLEIGH ESTATE CLASSIC CUVÉE 2009, WEST DORSET £25
Chardonnay, Pinot Noir, Pinot Meunier 12%

WHITES

MAS ROBERT VIC WHITE 2011, SOUTHERN FRANCE £6.59
Blend of Vermentino, Chardonnay,
Sauvignon Blanc, Muscat 12.5%

PARVA RES CATARRATTO 2011, SICILY £7.25
Catarratto 12.5%

CALUSARI PINOT GRIGIO 2012, ROMANIA £7.49
Pinot Gris 12.5%

VINA PALACIEGA RIOJA 2011, RIOJA, SPAIN £8.23
Viura 12.5%

PAUL BUISSE TOURAINE 2012, LOIRE, FRANCE £8.30
Sauvignon Blanc 12.5%

DOMAINE DE GUILLEMARINE, PICPOUL 2011, LANGUEDOC, FRANCE £9.40
Piquepoul Blanc 13%

CHAMONIX BLANC 2011, FRANSCHHOEK VALLEY, SOUTH AFRICA £9.75
Chardonnay, Sauvignon Blanc,
Chenin Blanc 12%

KARL JOHNER 2011, GERMANY £10.75
Rivaner 13.5%

ALAN GEOFFROY CHARDONNAY 2011, BURGUNDY, FRANCE £10.75
Chardonnay 12.5%

JULIAN SCHAAL CHARDONNAY 2011, ELGIN, SOUTH AFRICA £12.75
Chardonnay 13%

THE ARCHITECT 2011, EASTERN AUSTRALIA £13.50
Chardonnay 12.1%

AURAMARIS VEMENTINO 2011, TUSCANY, ITALY £13.60
Vermentino, Grechetto 13.5%

DELIVERY & CONTACT

GREAT WINE IS ONLY A GULP AWAY...

Free delivery on orders worth £100 or more.

Standard delivery £8.50 (3 working days) on orders under £100 to mainland UK.

For other destinations please visit the website for more information.

This list is correct at the time of printing it will be changing continuously, for the most up-to-date pricelist, please visit us online.

www.gulpwines.com

Sorbet
LIVING

Cookbook photo shoot prop supplier!

Sorbet Living is the creation of History of Art graduate, Debbie Gent. Debbie worked as a Tailoring Buyer for high street labels Next and Bhs. On buying trips to Paris, New York and Florence, Debbie developed a passion for searching out unusual 'homeware'.

Her first 'Beach House Collection' of lighting and tableware was launched in 2002 through independents. Her brand has developed into a unique range of ceramics, glassware, lighting and wallpaper with a contemporary country feel which is available online and through selected retailers. The Sorbet brand favours a 'handmade' look, quirky but functional, eclectic and beautiful.

Sorbet Living products have been featured by many publications, including Country Living, The Telegraph, House Beautiful, The Evening standard and Ideal Home magazine to name a few.

www.sorbetliving.com

BLOOMINGVILLE

*Bloomingville®
– ever changing homes

Cookbook photo shoot prop supplier!

Bloomingville create, discover and collect beautiful objects for the home and garden.

Bloomingville A/S was founded in Denmark in 2000. From its modest beginnings with only 2 employees it has developed into a thriving business with a team of 40 employees and 40 agents in Europe. Throughout this growth process it has maintained its focus on excellent quality, reasonable prices and the highest level of service. In June 2011, Initially, Bloomingville's product line consisted of items sourced from European producers as well as a small variety of pieces designed by the company's founder, Betina Stampe. Over time, that focus shifted and today the vast majority of the products are designed in-house, supplemented by special vintage items sourced directly from selected suppliers in Southeast Asia and Africa. The unique Bloomingville style is a mixture of raw products with a nostalgic Scandinavian twist and reproductions of fantastic pieces from times past inspired by French brocante.

www.bloomingville.co.uk

SOUTHEND FARM BARNS

The Barns at Southend Farm in Chichester is a wedding venue like no other...

Set in stunning countryside, our converted farm buildings and beautiful landscaped gardens are built and run using the latest environmentally sustainable technology.

Owners William and Mariella Fleming are building on a proud history of green credentials at Southend Farm. The Fleming family have been leading the way with environmentally-friendly farming here for over half a century. Today, they continue to be devoted to sustainable management of the land, trees and hedgerows, encouraging wildlife like deer, hares and bees.

What's more, the Flemings know how to throw a serious party. They can help make your wedding ceremony and reception the kind of event people will talk about for years to come.

Southend Farm is also available for parties, events and courses.

www.southendfarms.co.uk www.facebook.com/SouthendBarns

ATELIER OF ALCHEMY

ATELIER
OF ALCHEMY

Atelier of Alchemy is the latest creative services offering from Molly Morris, founder of the boutique interactive design studio, **The Neon Hive.**

As a former Brand Manager within the LVMH Group, Molly's latest venture, **Atelier of Alchemy,** is a dedicated brand consultancy for start-up brands. With over 15 years experience in niche, esoteric and luxury goods brand marketing, on both client and agency sides, she really understands the importance of strong communication design — especially when an artisan or independent brand is just starting out in such a competitive marketplace.

Whatever the scale of your business, astute and professional graphic design can give you the edge over your competitors. In an age of visual overload, decreasing attention spans and increasingly discerning customers, it's the little nuances that speak volumes — great design is ALWAYS in the details.

Atelier of Alchemy takes great pride in helping to create brands and seeing them evolve and succeed by embracing the brand's vision. Brand alchemy, the daily practice of art, design and creative marketing.

www.atelierofalchemy.com
www.theneonhive.com @theneonhive

THE BEST LITTLE CHEFS I KNOW!

The kitchen is a great place to experiment with food...

Children ages one to five are notoriously picky eaters and inviting them into the kitchen to cook helps expose them to new tastes.

Let them listen to the whir of the mixer, knead the dough and watch it rise, smell it baking and taste the bread warm, fresh from the oven...

If you have children I implore you to cook in the kitchen with them from a young age - just let them get messy!

THE RARE BRAND MARKET LARDER

As well as offering this book as an i-Pad version we plan to start selling the foods found within this cookbook online at:

www.therarebrandmarketlarder.co.uk

We also plan to offer a range of cookbook related product items to buy as gifts for foodie people in your lives or just you!

Please go to the website above to find out more about these extra products that sit alongside this book or follow us on Twitter:

@therarebrandlarder

Behind the scenes...

We had a great time tasting all of the recipes during the photo shoot - what a tough job... but someone had to do it!

Om, nom, nom!

NOTES TO READER

- Essential oils are highly concentrated and very potent, so avoid using when pregnant and never use on children. Always dilute the oil in a carrier oil like olive oil, grapeseed or almond and never apply pure undiluted oil directly to skin.

- Both metric and imperial measurements have been given in this book. Use one set of measurements only and not a mixture of both.

- Preheat ovens before use and cook on the centre shelf wherever possible. If using a fan oven, reduce the heat by 10-20°C, but check with your handbook.

- This book contains recipes made with nuts. Those with known allergic reactions to nuts and nut derivatives, pregnant and breast feeding women and very young children should avoid these dishes.

- Dishes containing raw or partially cooked eggs should not be served to those with weak or compromised immune systems, such as pregnant women, the elderly or the very young.

- Leftovers, if to be kept, should be covered and refrigerated or frozen as soon as cool and kept no longer than indicated. Never pre-heat previously frozen or re-heated food.

- Always be sure to read a recipe right through before starting to cook.

COOK'S NOTES

COOK'S NOTES